PRINCIPLES OF
ECONOMICS

STUDENT GUIDE

compiled by Iris F. Hartley, FLMI

To accompany the textbook,
Principles of Economics
by Thomas J. Hailstones
D. J. O'Conor Professor of Economics
Xavier University, Cincinnati

FLMI Insurance Education Program
Life Management Institute LOMA
Atlanta, Georgia

The **Life Office Management Association** is a research and educational association of life and health insurance companies operating in the United States, Canada, and a number of other countries. Among its activities is the sponsorship of an educational program intended primarily for home office and branch office employees of these companies.

The **FLMI Insurance Education Program** is comprised of Level I, "Fundamentals of Life and Health Insurance," and Level II, "Functional Aspects of Life and Health Insurance." Upon the completion of Level I, the student is awarded a Certificate. Upon the completion of both levels, the student is designated a Fellow of the Life Management Institute (FLMI) and is awarded a Diploma.

Project Editor: Brian K. McGreevy. J.D., FLMI
Production Editor: Dani L. Long, FLMI

ISBN 0-915322-71-4

Printed in the United States of America

Preface

LOMA has prepared this Student Guide for use in conjunction with <u>Principles of Economics</u> by Thomas J. Hailstones. This workbook is intended to help students prepare for the FLMI examination.

This Guide, like all LOMA Student Guides, is designed solely as a STUDY AID. It is not a substitute for reading and studying the text, because the examination is based on the textbook and not on the Student Guide.

Each chapter in the Student Guide is keyed directly to the textbook. There is a consistent format for all of the chapters in the Guide, and each chapter section has a distinct purpose. The purpose of each of these chapter sections is as follows:

> (1) The OBJECTIVES section presents the student with a list of specific learning objectives covering the knowledge expected of the student when he or she has completed the chapter.

> (2) The WORKING OUTLINE section provides a detailed review of each chapter and reinforces those concepts presented in the text. The major portion of the working outline prompts the student for answers to fill-in-the-blank questions. This procedure encourages the student to read the textbook carefully, looking for the specific information needed to fill in the blanks. When correctly completed, this outline can be of great assistance in the student's study and review for the examination. In addition, the working outline contains matching exercises which give the students practice answering questions based on the text material and using the concepts presented in the chapter. Although the majority of the questions asked in the working outline can be answered by referring to the text, some, notably those which require the student to draw conclusions based on various examples, cannot be answered soley by reading the text. In such cases, the working outline is followed by a section called SELECTED ANSWERS TO WORKING OUTLINE.

(3) The TERMINOLOGY AND CONCEPTS INTRODUCED section
lists some of the key words and phrases used in the
chapter and allows the student to test his or her grasp
of the material by writing out the definitions of these
key words and phrases in the blanks provided.

(4) and (5) The SAMPLE OBJECTIVE QUESTIONS and their
ANALYSES provide the student with practice questions
typical of those found on FLMI examinations. Each
question in this section is answerable from the text.
The correct answer to each question is also provided
along with the reason(s) the alternative answer choices
for each question are incorrect.

(6) The REVIEW QUESTIONS test the student's general
knowledge of concepts presented in each chapter. Most
of these questions are answerable from the text, and no
other reference is necessary. Answers to those
questions which cannot be answered directly from the
text are given in the section titled ANSWERS TO SELECTED
REVIEW QUESTIONS. Review questions generally require
short essay answers.

Contents

The Nature and Scope of Economics

OBJECTIVES

In this chapter, you will be introduced to the science of economics, and you will see how economics is similar to other sciences. You will study the definition of economics, and you will be exposed to the areas of study within the broad field of economics. Upon completion of this chapter, you should be able to

- Name and describe the four types of utility

- Define each of the four factors of production

- Explain what is meant by functional distribution of income

- List the characteristics of economic goods and economic services

- Distinguish between wealth and income

- Explain why economists sometimes disagree

- Differentiate between economic theory and economic policy

- Contrast microeconomics and macroeconomics

WORKING OUTLINE

I.   ECONOMICS DEFINED

1. What is economics? _____

_____

_____

Economics and Production

2. Define each of the following terms:

   ● Production--_____

   _____

   _____

   ● Utility--_____

   _____

3. The four most frequently recognized utilities are listed below. For each utility, tell <u>when</u> it occurs and give an example of it.

   (1) Form utility-- _____

   _____

   _____

   (2) Place utility-- _____

   _____

   _____

   (3) Time utility-- _____

   _____

   _____

   (4) Possession utility-- _____

   _____

   _____

4. _____ utility applies only to products, but _____,

   _____, and _____ utility apply to both

   services and products.

Economics and Distribution

5. In the study of economics, the term <u>distribution</u> refers to the

    _____ of the total product among _____

    _____.

6. Before a person or business can engage in the production of goods

    or services, certain prerequisites or corequisites, known as

    _____, are necessary.

7. Define <u>labor</u>. _____

    _____

    ● Labor includes both physical and mental application by both

      _____ and _____ workers.

    ● Labor includes the application of human effort for _____

      _____ as well as the production of goods.

8. In economics, the term <u>land</u> does not include _____

    but it does include all _____

    _____.

9. Define <u>capital</u>. _____

    _____

    ● Capital does not include _____

      _____

    ● Is money considered to be capital? _____ Explain your answer.

      _____

      _____

3

10. Define _entrepreneur_. _____

    _____

    ● Entrepreneurship is the factor of production which _____

      _____.

11. According to the functional distribution of income theory,
    remuneration is made to each factor of production. The factors
    of production appear in the left-hand column below. In the blank
    beside each factor of production, write the letter from the
    right-hand column which identifies the type of remuneration which
    is distributed to that factor.

    _____(1) Labor   a. Interest

    _____(2) Land   b. Profit

    _____(3) Capital   c. Rent

    _____(4) Entrepreneurship   d. Wages

12. The functional distribution of income theory is a product of

    a(n) _____ economic environment.

13. Although it is impossible for every factor to increase its

    relative share of the total product, all factors can have a

    larger _____ by contributing to an increase in

    the _____. Thus, _____ from

    various sources are the means of improving the return to all

    factors.

14. Differentiate between _positive economics_ and _normative economics_.

    _____

    _____

Economics and Consumption

15. Consumption is the _____ of a good or service. Explain the difference between the consumption of gasoline and the consumption of automobile tires. _____

    _____

    _____

16. Explain the importance of consumption to economics. _____

    _____

    _____

Goods and Services

17. To be an economic good, an object must be

    (1) _____   (3) _____

    (2) _____   (4) _____

18. Are ideas considered economic goods? _____ Why or why not?

    _____

19. Give an example of how the usefulness of a commodity can change.

    _____

    _____

20. Which two characteristics of economic goods determine the value or price of an item? _____ and _____

21. What does the term "transferable" mean when used to describe an object? _____

22. Economic services are _____ activities that

    are _____, _____, and _____.

23. The three principal types of goods are economic goods, free
    goods, and public goods. We have already defined economic goods.
    Define each of the other two terms.

    ● Free goods--_____

      _____

    ● Public goods-- _____

      _____

24. The category of economic goods can be subdivided as follows:

    (1) Consumer goods, which are those _____

        _____, and

    (2) Capital goods, which are those _____

        _____.

25. Wealth is the sum total of _____

    _____.

26. Estimates of the total wealth of the United States and Canada
    vary widely. Give three sources from which these differences
    arise.

    (1) _____

    (2) _____

    (3) _____

27. Some experts measure wealth by totaling the assets of the
    individuals and the firms of an economy; others add to this the

    _____ .

28. What are two common practices for valuing natural resources?

    (1) _____

    (2) _____

29. Describe the relationship between money and wealth. _____

    _____

    _____

30. Why do economists feel that some intangibles should be included
    in a count of wealth while others should be excluded?

    _____

    _____

    _____

31. Define income. _____

    _____ How does income differ

    from wealth? _____

    _____

32. Is a nation's total wealth increased annually by the total amount

    of its annual income? _____ Why or why not? _____

    _____

    _____

33. The value of goods and services produced is known as _____,

while the dollars derived from the production of goods and

services are known as _____.

34. Give one argument in favor of channeling a portion of national
output into the form of machinery, equipment, and technology.

_____

_____

_____

II. ECONOMICS IS RELATED TO OTHER SCIENCES

1. Explain how the science of economics relates to each of the
following sciences:

- Physics-- _____

- Political science-- _____

- Sociology-- _____

- Psychology-- _____

- Philosophy-- _____

- Mathematics-- _____

- Logic-- _____

Prudential Judgment

2. Use the concept of prudential judgment to explain why two

economists, applying the rules of logic, can disagree on the

solution to one problem. _____

_____

_____

III. ECONOMIC THEORY VERSUS ECONOMIC POLICY

1. Differentiate between economic theory and economic policy.

   _____

   _____

   _____

2. Give an example of a situation in which economic policy does not
   follow economic theory. _____

   _____

   _____

IV. MICROECONOMICS AND MACROECONOMICS

1. Each of the statements below applies to either the field of
   microeconomics or macroeconomics. In the blank in front of each
   statement, fill in the field of study described in the statement.

   _____ (1) Suggests ways and means of obtaining a high
                       level of employment

   _____ (2) Deals with the general price level

   _____ (3) Deals with the principle of supply and
                       demand

   _____ (4) Formulates ideas on monetary and fiscal
                       policy as a means of stabilizing the
                       economy

   _____ (5) Endeavors to discover what motivates the
                       individual to spend or save

9

TERMINOLOGY AND CONCEPTS INTRODUCED

economics-- _____

_____

production--_____

_____

utility--_____

_____

form utility--_____

_____

place utility--_____

_____

time utility--_____

_____

possession utility--_____

_____

distribution--_____

_____

factors of production--_____

_____

labor--_____

_____

land--_____

_____

capital--_____

_____

entrepreneur--_____

_____

positive economics--_____

_____

normative economics--_____

_____

consumption--_____

_____

economic good--_____

_____

material--_____

_____

useful--_____

_____

scarce--_____

_____

transferable--_____

_____

economic services--_____

_____

free good--_____

_____

public good--_____

_____

consumer goods--_____

_____

capital goods--_____

_____

wealth--_____

_____

income--_____

_____

real income--_____

_____

money income--_____

_____

prudential judgment--_____

_____

economic theory--_____

_____

economic policy--_____

_____

microeconomics--_____

_____

macroeconomics--_____

_____

SAMPLE OBJECTIVE QUESTIONS

1. An economist's definition of land as one of the factors of production generally would include the following resources:

   A. Chemicals
   B. Timber
   C. Buildings
   D. Oil

      (1) All of these
      (2) A, B and D only
      (3) A and D only
      (4) B and C only
      (5) B and D only

2. In economics, goods can be classified as economic goods, free goods, or public goods. In this context, a public good is one which

      (1) lacks the element of scarcity and therefore has no price
      (2) is transferable, but not material, useful, or scarce
      (3) costs the supplier nothing, but carries a price paid by the user in addition to any taxes
      (4) is material, useful, scarce, and transferable to the supplier, but is without direct price to the user

3. Microeconomics is concerned in part with

      (1) monetary policies
      (2) the principle of supply and demand
      (3) the total employment level
      (4) the general price level

ANALYSIS OF SAMPLE OBJECTIVE QUESTIONS

1. Choice (2) is the correct answer; statements A, B, and D are all correct. Statement C is incorrect because buildings are included in the definition of capital, not in the definition of land.

2. The correct answer is choice (4). Choices (1), (2), and (3) are all incorrect. Choice (1) is the definition of a free good, while choice (3) is the opposite of the definition of a public good. Choice (2) is incorrect because a public good exhibits all four of these characteristics from the supplier's point of view.

3. The correct answer is choice (2). Choices (1), (3), and (4) are the subject matter of macroeconomics.

REVIEW QUESTIONS

1. Explain why economics is considered a science. How does the study of economics compare to the study of physical sciences?

2. How does form utility differ from place, time, and possession utility?

3. The economic definition for each of the four factors of production-- labor, land, capital, and entrepreneurship--specifies clearly what is and what is not included in that factor. Indicate the scope of each factor of production by giving examples of items that would or would not be included in that factor.

4. Contrast a self-sufficient barter economy with a more complex economy. How does the distribution of remuneration vary in these two economies?

5. In order to illustrate the difference between positive economics and normative economics, make two statements about the distribution of remuneration among the factors of production: let the first statement exemplify positive economics and let the second statement exemplify normative economics.

6. Describe the various uncertainties which make it difficult to measure wealth.

7. Is real income equivalent to money income? Explain your answer.

8. What correlation frequently exists between wealth and income?

9. What application does the concept of prudential judgment have in economics?

The Process of Economizing

2

OBJECTIVES

In this chapter, you will see how nations can economize. You will be introduced to the processes of specialization and exchange. The chapter concludes with a study of the principle of comparative advantage. Upon completion of this chapter, you should be able to

- Discuss why nations must economize

- Identify the factors of production for production on a national scale

- Explain how specialization and exchange can increase productivity

- State the limits of specialization

- Illustrate the principle of comparative advantage

WORKING OUTLINE

Introduction

1. Economizing is the process of applying _____

   in an endeavor to satisfy _____.

I. ECONOMIZING

1. Briefly describe the manner in which individuals economize.

   _____

   _____

Nations Must Economize

2. The total output and standard of living of any nation are dependent upon the extent of and the use of the factors of production. The terms for the factors of production when referring to them on a national scale are listed in the left-hand column below. In the blank beside each term, write the letter identifying the term in the right-hand column which is used to refer to that same factor of production on an individual scale.

    _____(1) Natural resources   a.   Capital

    _____(2) Population   b.   Entrepreneurship

    _____(3) Entrepreneurship   c.   Labor

    _____(4) Technological development   d.   Land

3. Generally, the larger the population of a given nation, the

    _____ is the total production of goods and services of

    that nation.

4. List seven other characteristics of a nation's population that influence total output.

    (1) _____   (5) _____

    (2) _____   (6) _____

    (3) _____   (7) _____

    (4) _____

5. The greater the amount of land and natural resources at the

    disposal of a nation, the greater _____

    _____.

6. National resources consist of

    (1) _____   (3) _____

    (2) _____   (4) _____

16

7. People can produce more with _____,

_____, and _____

than they can with manual labor alone.

8. The use of better machinery and equipment over the past decades has resulted in a continuous increase in the standard of living in most countries. Give four examples of technological developments that enhance the output of goods and services.

(1) _____

(2) _____

(3) _____

(4) _____

9. Leaders who possess _____ and _____ are a key

element in entrepreneurship on a national scale.

10. List four aspects of the economic system of a nation which influence the entrepreneurial activities of that nation.

(1) _____

(2) _____

(3) _____

(4) _____

II. SPECIALIZATION AND EXCHANGE

1. Productivity determines income, and income determines

_____. Therefore, a worth-

while goal for each individual or nation is to increase its

_____.

Nature of Specialization and Exchange

2. When an individual, a firm, a geographic area, or a nation specializes, it _____ instead of

_____ .

3. Define exchange. _____

_____

_____

4. An economy of specialization and exchange yields _____

_____ than an economy characterized by

self-sufficiency. Why is this so? _____

_____

Limits to Specialization and Exchange

5. In modern economies, the high degree of specialization and

exchange plays an important role in _____ .

6. The degree of specialization and exchange is limited by the

_____ , that is, it is not profitable to

engage in this process if the sale of items produced is

insufficient to _____

_____ or if one cannot

produce enough to _____

_____ .

7. Define division of labor. _____

_____

8. List three factors that affect the size of a market.

    (1) _____

    (2) _____

    (3) _____

III. LAW OF COMPARATIVE ADVANTAGE

Absolute Advantage

1. "Brazil has an absolute advantage over Canada in the production of coffee." In your own words, explain this statement.

    _____

    _____

Comparative Advantage

2. What is the principle of comparative advantage? _____

    _____

    _____

3. If the application of the principle of comparative advantage

    results in an increase in total production, both parties will

    benefit because of the process of _____.

An Example of Comparative Advantage Between Nations

Table 2-1 Production of Countries X and Y Before Specialization

Country	Iron Ore Productive Units Used	Pounds	Oil Productive Units Used	Gallons
X	2	20	3	60
Y	2	16	3	30
Total	4	36	6	90

19

4. Table 2-1 presents a hypothetical situation in which Country X has an absolute advantage over Country Y in the production of both iron ore and oil. According to this table, Country X should specialize in _____, for it has a _____ to _____ advantage in the production of this item over Country Y, while it has only a _____ to _____ advantage in the production of _____. (A)*

5. Complete Table 2-2 below, showing the effects of specialization according to the principle of comparative advantage. (A)

Table 2-2 Production After Specialization According to Principle of Comparative Advantage

	Iron Ore		Oil	
Country	Productive Units Used	Pounds	Productive Units Used	Gallons
X	_____	___	_____	___
Y	_____	___	_____	___
Total	_____	_____	_____	_____

6. What effect does this type of specialization have on the total production of iron ore? _____

Of oil? _____ (A)

7. Assume that Country X disregarded the principal of comparative advantage in selecting the product in which to specialize. Complete Table 2-3 showing what would happen if countries X and Y each specialized in the product they did not produce in Table 2-2. (A)

* indicates that the answer is given in this Student Guide

Table 2-3 Production After Specialization in "Wrong" Products

Country	Iron Ore Productive Units Used	Pounds	Oil Productive Units Used	Gallons
X	_____	____	_____	___
Y	_____	____	_____	___
Total	_____	_____	_____	_____

8. How does the total production of iron ore and oil under this method of specialization (illustrated in Table 2-3) compare with the method of specialization illustrated in Table 2-2? **(A)**

_____

_____

Comparative Advantage in Practice

9. A large portion of the sectional or regional trade within a nation and of the international trade throughout the world is based on the principle of comparative advantage. Give at least two examples. _____

_____

Limitations to Comparative Advantage

10. Give two reasons why regions or nations must be careful not to overspecialize.

(1) _____

(2) _____

11. How can the demands of the market influence the decision to
    specialize? _____

    _____

12. Explain how military considerations can limit the use of the
    principle of comparative advantage. _____

    _____

SELECTED ANSWERS TO WORKING OUTLINE

I.   ECONOMIZING

Nations Must Economize

2. (1)d; (2) c; (3) b; (4) a

III. LAW OF COMPARATIVE ADVANTAGE

An Example of Comparative Advantage Between Nations

4. oil; 2 to 1; 5 to 4; iron ore

5. Table 2-2 Completed

	Iron Ore		Oil	
Country	Productive Units Used	Pounds	Productive Units Used	Gallons
X	-	-	5	100
Y	5	40	-	-
Total	5	40	5	100

6. resulted in 4 additional pounds of iron ore and 10 additional
    gallons of oil

7. Table 2-3 Completed

| | Iron Ore | | | Oil | |
Country	Productive Units Used	Pounds		Productive Units Used	Gallons
X	5	50		-	-
Y	-	-		5	50
Total	5	50		5	50

8. 10 additional pounds of iron ore, but 50 fewer gallons of oil

TERMINOLOGY AND CONCEPTS INTRODUCED

economizing--_____

_____

population--_____

_____

natural resources--_____

_____

technological development--_____

_____

specialization--_____

_____

exchange--_____

_____

division of labor--_____

_____

absolute advantage--_____

_____

comparative advantage--_____

_____

principle of comparative advantage--_____

_____

SAMPLE OBJECTIVE QUESTIONS

1. The following table shows the production of wheat and rice in two hypothetical countries:

	WHEAT		RICE	
	Productive Units Used	Tons	Productive Units Used	Tons
Grainland	2	120	3	60
Heartland	2	100	3	30

Assuming no other factors are pertinent, if the principle of comparative advantage is applied in both countries, the following statements correctly describe this situation:

A. Grainland would have a greater comparative advantage in the production of rice than in the production of wheat
B. Heartland would have an absolute advantage in the production of wheat
C. If Grainland and Heartland specialize according to the principle of comparative advantage, the two countries would produce a greater total amount of both rice and wheat than they presently produce
D. If Grainland and Heartland engaged in trade, Grainland would import wheat and Heartland would import rice

   (1) All of these
   (2) A, C and D only
   (3) B, C and D only
   (4) A and C only
   (5) A and D only

2. In an economy of specialization and exchange, it is generally true that

    A. Total production is likely to be greater than in an economy characterized by self-sufficiency

    B. Total income is likely to be higher than in an economy characterized by self-sufficiency

    C. The degree to which the economy can benefit from specialization and exchange is limited by the size of the market

    D. A high degree of specialization reduces the economy's vulnerability to business recessions

        (1) All of these
        (2) A, B and C only
        (3) B, C and D only
        (4) A and B only
        (5) A and D only

ANALYSIS OF SAMPLE OBJECTIVE QUESTIONS

1. The correct answer is choice (2). Statement B is wrong because Grainland has an absolute advantage over Heartland in the production of both wheat and rice. Statement A is correct; Grainland has a greater comparative advantage in the production of rice. If both countries specialize according to the principle of comparative advantage, they will produce a total of 250 tons of rice and 100 tons of wheat; therefore, statement C is correct. Statement D is correct; if Grainland produces rice, it will have to import wheat, and if Heartland produces wheat, it will have to import rice.

2. Choice (2) is the correct answer; statements A, B, and C are correct. Statement D is false because a nation with a high degree of specialization is particularly vulnerable to business recessions.

REVIEW QUESTIONS

1. Why do individuals find it necessary to economize? What causes nations to economize?

2. How does specialization affect productivity?

3. Using the figures in the table below, explain how one producer with an absolute advantage over another producer in the production of two commodities can select the best commodity in which to specialize.

Table 2-4 Production of Bull and Bear Before Specialization

| | Commodity #1 | | Commodity #2 | |
Producer	Productive Units Used	Number	Productive Units Used	Number
Bull	4	60	3	15
Bear	4	40	3	12
Total	8	100	6	27

4. Assume that Bull (in Table 2-4) specializes in the commodity in which it has the greatest comparative advantage, and that Bull and Bear agree to divide evenly the increase in production that results from such specialization. How much of Commodity #1 and Commodity #2 do Bull and Bear each have after the specialization?

5. What factors limit the use of the principle of comparative advantage?

The Economic System

OBJECTIVES

In this chapter, you will study the functioning of a free enterprise capitalistic system and the roles of competition and government intervention in such a system. You will become acquainted with the types of business firms. You also will learn the primary economic goals of the United States and Canada. Upon completion of this chapter, you should be able to

- Explain the importance of competition in a capitalistic system

- Identify the aspects of a capitalistic system that affect the remuneration paid to the factors of production

- Describe the various types of business firms

- Explain why and how governments must sometimes intervene in the business community

- Discuss the principle of subsidiarity

- List primary and supplementary economic goals

- Contrast market economics to command economies

WORKING OUTLINE

I. **FREE ENTERPRISE CAPITALISM**

1. In a free enterprise capitalistic system (also know as a(n)

    _____), decisions as to what and how much to

    produce and the manner in which goods and services are to be

    allocated are made primarily by _____.

● Name two other types of economic systems.

(1) _____ (2) _____

● How are such decisions made in these types of economies? _____

_____

2. The institution of _____ is essential to a capitalistic

system. What is the full significance of this concept? _____

_____

_____

_____

3. Define the term profit. _____

_____

_____

● Give the equation for computing profit.

Profit = _____

● Profit is the incentive for obtaining and using _____

to produce _____ that satisfy consumer

needs.

4. Individuals in the free enterprise system can sell productive

services to another or they can combine several _____

_____ to produce goods and sell them at a profit.

5. To operate a business, individuals must produce goods or services

that _____ and must offer them at

_____.

6. How does a producer increase the well-being of other people by

   using property to make a profit for itself? _____

   _____

7. In a capitalistic economic system, both the ultimate use of

   _____and the allocation of_____

   are determined primarily by consumer demand. Generally, other

   things being equal, the stronger the demand for a particular good

   or service, _____.

8. What would happen in a model economy if the demand for total
   goods and services were so large that there were not enough
   labor, resources, and capital to produce all of them? _____

   _____

   _____

The Role of Competition

9. In a command economy, a centralized authority assigns _____

   _____ to firms and directs _____

   to employment in various industries.

   ● A(n) _____ system, on the other

     hand, relies on competition to regulate the volume of _____

     and the allocation of _____.

10. If competition in a capitalistic system is effective, the economy
    functions efficiently without an overseer. How does competition
    protect the following parties?

    ● Consumers--_____

      _____

● Resource owners and workers--_____

_____

● Business firms--_____

_____

11. Even in a free enterprise capitalistic economy, some business
firms may gain substantial control over the price, output, and
employment conditions in a certain industry. In such situations,
it is considered the responsibility of government to _____
_____, but not to assume ownership of the _____
_____.

12. What is the guiding principle of competitive capitalism? _____
_____
_____

13. In a system of competitive capitalism, the government should
influence or control production only in situations where it is
believed that _____
_____--as in the case of _____
or _____.

14. What is meant by laissez faire? _____
_____ How does a government
maintain a policy of laissez faire? _____
_____

Price as a Rationing Mechanism

15. How do supply and price influence decisions of what and how much will be produced? _____

    _____

    _____

16. In a capitalistic system, other things being equal, the use of resources and human energy is determined by _____

    _____. This process can be described as both democratic and nondemocratic. Explain. _____

    _____

    _____

    _____

17. Individual consumers determine, in part, the _____ paid to the various factors of production in that _____

    _____ provides business with the means by which they can obtain labor, land, and capital to

    _____.

18. In a model system, each factor of production is remunerated according to its _____ toward the commodity or service being produced.

    • This _____, in turn, is measured by the _____ that the firm is willing to pay for that factor.

31

● The _____ the firm is willing to pay for each

factor is limited by _____.

19. The income of a factor of production is also affected by the

_____ and _____ of that

factor.

II. BUSINESS FIRMS

1. In a capitalistic economy, business firms facilitate the
   process by which the following are determined:

   (1) _____

   (2) _____

   (3) _____

2. Production for the purpose of satisfying consumer demand in a

   capitalistic economy usually is undertaken by _____

   _____.

Types of Business Firms

3. What is a sole proprietorship (single proprietorship)? _____

   _____

4. Describe two advantages and three disadvantages of the sole
   proprietorship form of business.

   Advantages--

   (1) _____

   (2) _____

Disadvantages--

(1) _____

_____

(2) _____

_____

(3) _____

_____

5. A partnership is an association of two or more persons to

carry on as _____ a business for profit. The

partnership is usually found in small businesses that require

_____ and in professions such as

_____.

6. State two advantages of the partnership over the sole
proprietorship.

(1) _____

(2) _____

7. Which two disadvantages of the sole proprietorship are also found
in the partnership form of business?

(1) _____

(2) _____

8. Describe any additional disadvantages of the partnership.

_____

_____

33

9. A corporation is a separate legal entity apart from its owners. Name three things a corporation can do because of its status as a "legal person:"

(1) _____

(2) _____

(3) _____

10. List six advantages of the corporate form of business.

(1) _____

(2) _____

(3) _____

(4) _____

(5) _____

(6) _____

11. Explain the double taxation that is levied on corporate income.

_____

_____

12. State three disadvantages, other than double taxation, of the corporate form of business.

(1) _____

(2) _____

(3) _____

13. A cooperative is owned primarily by _____

_____.

14. A cooperative may be incorporated and pay dividends to its stock-
    holders. How does such a cooperative differ from a traditional
    corporation? _____

    _____

15. A major difference between a cooperative and other forms of

    business enterprise is that the cooperative's net income, after

    payment of _____,

    is distributed among _____,

    on a pro rata basis according to _____

    _____

16. Although consumer cooperatives are popular in Canada and in many

    European countries, they have not achieved prominence in the

    United States. State one reason for this lack of acceptance or

    success. _____

    _____

17. List three major types of cooperatives.

    (1) _____ (3) _____

    (2) _____

III. COMPETITION IN THE ECONOMY

1. Competition is the _____ of the free enterprise

   economic system.

   ● State three ways that producers compete for the business of
     individual buyers.

     (1) _____ (3) _____

     (2) _____

● Competition among producers restricts one firm from _____

_____.

● How do producers benefit from competition among consumers?

_____

● State four benefits to consumers of competition among producers.

(1) _____

(2) _____

(3) _____

(4) _____

2. What types of freedoms are provided by competition?

_____

_____

_____

Competition and Monopoly

3. The degree of competition within and between economies varies

greatly. Cite potential reasons for such variations. _____

_____

_____

Government Regulated Markets

4. Public utilities are an example of a service that is regulated to

some degree by _____ so that

the market may be more orderly and may operate to the best

interest of the _____.

5. A public utility receives a franchise that gives the firm

_____ and gives the

applicable public service commission _____

_____ .

6. List five examples of government regulation of markets in the
   United States and/or Canada.

   (1) _____

   (2) _____

   (3) _____

   (4) _____

   (5) _____

7. Name three corporations owned by the Canadian government which
   provide services in competition with privately-owned businesses.

   (1) _____   (2) _____

   (3) _____

8. Describe an instance in which the United States government has

   entered a business indirectly. _____

   _____

Mixed Economy

9. The economies of Canada and the United States are mixed

   economies. What is a mixed economy? _____

   _____

37

10. Historically, the role of the government in the economies of the United States and Canada has been one of _____. In the past few decades, however, there has been a tendency to move in the direction of _____.

11. Describe the benefits provided by each of the following examples of government intervention:

   ● The United States Social Security Act--_____

   _____

   _____

   ● The Canada/Quebec Pension Plans and the Old Age Security Pension Act--_____

   _____

   _____

Subsidiary Role of Government

12. One well-regarded law of social philosophy which can be used as a criterion to determine the need for government intervention is known as the principle of _____ and is based on the concept that the community and the state are _____to the _____.

13. Explain the implications of this principle. _____

   _____

   _____

   _____

14. The principle of subsidiarity helps to protect _____

_____ and to maintain some degree of _____.

15. Give some examples of government intervention that are justified

by the principle of subsidiarity. _____

_____

IV. **GOALS FOR THE ECONOMY**

1. List four primary economic goals for the economies of the United
States and Canada.

(1) _____ (3) _____

(2) _____ (4) _____

2. What are four other goals that supplement these primary goals?

(1) _____ (3) _____

(2) _____ (4) _____

Full Employment

3. Define the following terms.

● Full employment-- _____

_____

● Frictional unemployment-- _____

_____

4. How has the definition of <u>full employment</u> changed in the

recent past? _____

_____

Stable Prices

5. Stable prices are said to exist when the Consumer Price Index,

which measures _____, moves

_____ percent, or less, _____ during

_____.

6. What two elements of the economy are substantially affected by
unstable prices?

(1) _____ (2) _____

Economic Growth

7. Why is it important for an economy's total output to grow each

year? _____

_____

_____

8. What are three ill effects of maintaining a level amount of
output each year?

(1) _____ (3) _____

(2) _____

9. In order to maintain or increase the existing standard of living

and to prevent _____ from rising or

_____ from occurring, it is necessary to

increase the _____ continuously, unless,

of course, workers are content to take the benefits of

_____ in the form of shorter working hours

instead of _____.

Balance of Payments Equilibrium

10. The goal for both the United States and Canada is to have the

   value of efforts equal to _____

   so that the _____ is in balance

   and the international values of _____

   remain stable.

V.   COMMAND ECONOMIES

1. List five disadvantages of capitalism.

   (1) _____   (4) _____

   (2) _____   (5) _____

   (3) _____

2. In command economies, there is a high degree of government

   _____ or _____ of the factors

   of production.

TERMINOLOGY AND CONCEPTS INTRODUCED

   free enterprise capitalistic system (market economy)--_____

   _____

   private property--_____

   _____

   profit--_____

   _____

   competition--_____

   _____

   laissez faire--_____

   _____

sole proprietorship--_____

_____

partnership--_____

_____

corporation--_____

_____

cooperative--_____

_____

franchise--_____

_____

mixed economy--_____

_____

principle of subsidiarity--_____

_____

full employment--_____

_____

frictional unemployment--_____

_____

command economies--_____

_____

SAMPLE OBJECTIVE QUESTIONS

1. A cooperative is a type of business enterprise owned primarily by the people who use it or buy from it. A distinctive characteristic of the cooperative is that its net income (after the payment of any dividend) is distributed to its

    (1) customers in equal shares, regardless of their respective volumes of purchases from the business
    (2) customers on a pro rata basis, according to their respective volumes of purchases from the business
    (3) shareholders on a pro rata basis, according to the number of shares owned
    (4) shareholders in equal shares, regardless of the number of shares owned

2. Country X has a capitalistic economy that is generally regulated by the force of competition, although some government regulation is typically applied in industries where competition does not provide effective regulation. Country X's economic system is correctly described as a

    (1) command economy
    (2) pure market economy
    (3) socialist economy
    (4) mixed economy

3. To judge the suitable extent of interaction between higher and lower economic units, economists often apply the principle of subsidiarity. The principle of subsidiarity implies that

    (1) lower economic units should receive certain economic benefits in exchange for subordinating their particular interests to the interests of a higher economic unit
    (2) a higher economic unit should incorporate lower economic units into its policy-making body so as to meet needs at all levels
    (3) a higher economic unit should not take on a function that lower economic units can perform for themselves
    (4) lower economic units should yield to the authority of a higher economic unit in cases of conflicting economic goals

4. At any given time, workers who are temporarily laid off, are in transit from one part of the country to another, or have quit or been fired account for a percentage of the unemployed in an economy. Unemployment that is attributed to these factors is categorized as

    (1) frictional unemployment
    (2) underemployment
    (3) cyclical unemployment
    (4) marginal unemployment

ANALYSIS OF SAMPLE OBJECTIVE QUESTIONS

1. Choice (2) is the correct answer. The net income of a cooperative is not distributed to the shareholders (3 and 4). When the net income is divided among the cooperative's customers, it is not apportioned evenly (1), but in accordance with the volume of purchases made by each customer.

2. The correct answer is choice (4); choices (1), (2), and (3) are all incorrect. As described, Country X is a mixed economy because it is characterized by competition that is not perfect, since some industries are regulated only by competition, while others require government regulation.

3. The correct answer is choice (3). Choices (1), (2), and (4) are all incorrect. The principle of subsidiarity states that each higher economic unit exists to give assistance to lower economic units. If the higher unit intervenes and performs functions that could be performed by lower units, the lower units lose part of their reason for existence.

4. Choice (1) is the correct answer; choices (2), (3), and (4) are all incorrect. At full employment, 95 percent of the civilian labor force is employed. Frictional unemployment is the 5 percent of the labor force who are expected to be unemployed even under the best of circumstances. These are workers who are out of work for reasons such as those listed in the question.

REVIEW QUESTIONS

1. In a model capitalistic economic system, a producer, in the process of using property to make a profit, will increase the well-being of other people. What are some of the possible outcomes in a situation that could not be considered "model"?

2. Under what circumstances is the government in a free enterprise capitalistic economy expected to exercise its authority over business firms? What action is the government to take at such times?

3. Describe and give examples of the various levels of government regulated markets.

4

The Circular Flow of Economic Activity

OBJECTIVES

In this chapter, you will study the continuous cycle of demand, production, income, and new demand and the model used to represent this circular flow. You will observe the impact of government spending on economic activity. Finally, you will learn to distinguish among the types of inflation. Upon completion of this chapter, you should be able to

- Illustrate graphically the elements of the circular flow of economic activity

- Discuss the effect on the economy of the various relationships between planned investment and planned saving

- Explain why a balanced budget tends to have a neutral effect on economic activity

- Describe the likely results of a government's spending more or less than it collects in taxes

- Identify the types of inflation

- Define stagflation

WORKING OUTLINE

Introduction

1. Owners of the factors of production perform services for business

   firms in exchange for payments. These payments become

   _____ to the owners of the productive factors. This

   _____ is used as_____ with which

   these owners buy goods and services.

2. The _____ that entrepreneurs or businesses

receive become _____ with which

they can buy goods or secure additional _____.

3. The continuous operation of _____, _____,

_____, and _____ creates the

circular flow of economic activity.

4. The circular flow of economic activity is the mechanism by which
the individuals and firms in the economy determine

(1) _____

(2) _____

(3) _____

I. CIRCULAR FLOW DEMONSTRATED

1. In a simplified model of the circular flow, the economy is

divided into two segments--_____ and

_____.

2. Individuals, including the owners of businesses, use their money

to buy _____.

3. Under what circumstances would all the goods and services

produced be sold? _____

_____

4. If all the goods and services produced are sold, businesses will

_____

_____.

5. The value of goods produced is determined by the cost of production--payments for _____, _____, and _____ in the form of _____, _____, and_____, plus the _____ for the entrepreneurs.

6. The total payment of income in the economy is equal to _____ _____ _____.

A Stable Economy

7. In order to preserve a stable economy, there must be additional spending from some source to make up for the amount of _____ in the economy. We can maintain a given level of economic activity only if there is an amount of _____ and/or _____ in the economy equal to the amount of _____.

8. In current economic analysis, spending on capital goods is referred to as _____.

9. As long as _____ equals _____ _____, there will be a stable flow of economic activity.

10. Under such circumstances, total actual _____ will equal total actual _____.

11. Since total _____ is a measure of total demand, and total _____ is equivalent to total production (_____), the demand for goods and services will equal the _____.

12. At any given time, actual _____ will equal actual _____.

13. When planned _____ is greater than planned _____, the economy will expand, causing _____ to increase until it comes into balance with _____.

14. If planned _____ is less than planned _____, the economy will contract, causing _____ to decrease until it comes into balance with _____.

A Contracting Economy

15. In the country of Aberdeen, planned $\underline{I}$ is $40,000 and planned $\underline{S}$ is $60,000. Therefore, Aberdeen's economy could be described as a(n)_____ economy.

16. This gap between planned $\underline{I}$ and planned $\underline{S}$ would produce a decrease in Aberdeen's level of economic activity. Most likely, this decrease would result in one or a combination of the following:

    (1) _____

    (2) _____

17. If the price of a unit produced in Aberdeen remains unchanged, then it is likely that Aberdeen businesses will experience an inventory accumulation. **(A)**

    A. Assume that Aberdeen businesses produced 100,000 units last year, but that only 90,000 units were purchased. Aberdeen businesses therefore accumulated _____ units in inventory last year.

    B. Assume that Aberdeen businesses now only expect to sell 90,000 units this year. Aberdeen businesses would reduce their production from the _____ units they produced last year to only 80,000 units this year. In this way, Aberdeen businesses will have the _____ units they desire for this year--_____ units from this year's production and _____ units from inventory.

    C. If Aberdeen businesses produce 20 percent fewer units this year, then they will use 20 percent less labor, land, and capital. Therefore, they will pay _____ percent less income to individuals. If the individuals in Aberdeen have less income to spend, there may be a further decline in business activity resulting in further _____.

18. Complete Figure 4-1 to represent Aberdeen's economy last year, given the assumptions made in #17 above. The price of each unit produced in Aberdeen is $2. **(A)**

49

Figure 4-1   Aberdeen's Contracting Economy--Inventory
              Accumulation

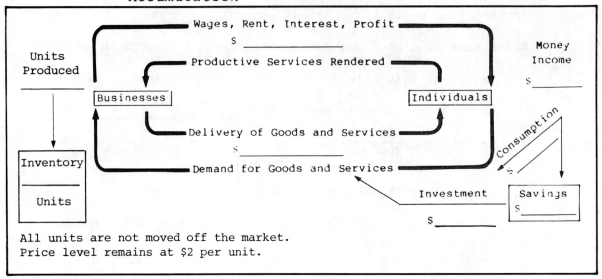

19. If the price of units produced in Aberdeen _____, then

    it is likely that Aberdeen businesses can move all units off the

    market even though planned S exceeds planned I.

    ● Aberdeen businesses were forced to lower prices because total

    _____ exceeded total _____.

    ● Lower prices result in weakened incentive to produce; therefore

    it is likely that the total output in the coming year will be

    _____.

    ● If businesses produce less, they will utilize fewer _____

    _____, individuals will receive less income,

    and total demand will _____.

20. Whenever planned I is less than planned S, as is the case in

    Aberdeen, total actual _____ will be less

    than total actual income, and total actual _____

    will be less than total actual supply.

- This will lead to _____ in subsequent periods because of inventory accumulation or falling prices or _____.
- As production is cut, _____ will fall, and this will reduce _____ and _____.

An Expanding Economy

21. In the country of Bailiwick, planned $\underline{I}$ is $80,000 and planned $\underline{S}$ is $60,000. Therefore, Bailiwick's economy could be described as a(n) _____ economy.

22. In Bailiwick, total spending exceeds total _____ and total demand exceeds total _____.

23. Because Bailiwick businesses receive more than they pay to the factors of production, there will most likely be an increase in _____ or an increase in _____ or a combination of both.

24. Complete Figure 4-2 to represent Bailiwick's economy last year, assuming that Bailiwick business produced 100,000 units last year and paid a total of $2 per unit in wages, rent, interest, and profit. **(A)**

25. Assume that Bailiwick businesses endeavor to increase production to satisfy the additional demand.

Figure 4-2 Bailiwick's Expanding Economy--Increase in Output and/or Price

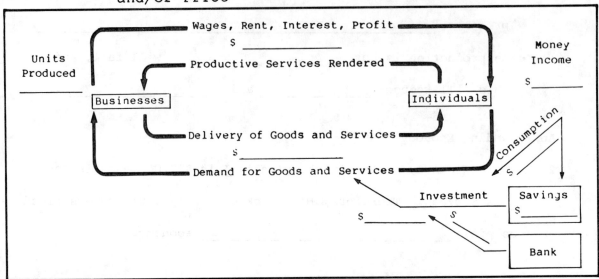

- The additional demand can be satisfied only if the Bailiwick

  economy is in a state of _____,

  that is, if _____, _____, _____,

  and _____ to increase production are available.

26. If individuals in Bailiwick receive higher incomes, they will

    increase _____, which will result in _____

    _____. As a result of the increased production,

    Bailiwick's economy will be operating at a higher level

    _____ and _____.

27. Assume that Bailiwick is in a state of full employment. The

    immediate result of planned I that exceeds planned S will be

    _____. Bailiwick businesses will

    be unable to obtain necessary _____ , _____,

    _____, and _____ to produce additional goods.

52

28. Under conditions of full employment, some businesses will endeavor to increase production to satisfy the additional _____ by bidding the necessary _____ away from other businesses. The bidding for relatively scarce _____ will force prices _____. Individuals will bid against each other for the limited goods available, thus spending more money to buy the same number of units.

29. Although the composition of production (the amount of _____ goods compared to the amount of _____ goods) may be changed, the _____ will not be changed in the short run.

30. Eventually, inflationary pressures can be alleviated if productivity can be increased through any of the following three measures:

    (1) _____

    (2) _____

    (3) _____

Summary of Circular Flow Model

31. Results of different relationships between investment (I) and savings (S) are listed in the numbered columns below. In the blank beside each numbered result, write the letter identifying the relationship of I to S that would produce this result in the economy.

        a. Planned I < planned S

        b. Planned I = planned S

        c. Planned I > planned S

_____ (1) If the economy is in a state of full employment, prices will tend to rise.

_____ (2) The level of economic activity will tend to decrease.

_____ (3) Prices will tend to decrease.

_____ (4) Prices will tend to remain stable.

_____ (5) If the economy is at less than full employment, the level of economic activity will tend to increase.

_____ (6) Economic activity will tend to have a stable flow.

II. GOVERNMENT AND THE CIRCULAR FLOW

1. At one time the primary function and objective of federal

    financing was to _____

    _____

    _____.

2. At this time, great emphasis was placed on _____

    _____.

3. In recent decades, Canada and the United States have used

    _____ as a means of stablizing the

    level of economic activity.

4. The examples of government activity that will be discussed in this section are based on the following three assumptions:

    (1) _____

    (2) _____

    _____

(3) _____

_____

A Balanced Budget

5. The effect of a balanced budget is that the government spends the

same amount as _____.

6. The taxes paid by _____ and _____

reduce their total spending, but the government spends the taxes

it collects, so the total spending remains the same. Thus, a

balanced budget <u>tends</u> to have a(n) _____ effect on the

economy.

7. A balanced budget might produce a change, however, in the

_____, insofar

as government spending would be substituted for some of the

_____ on consumption and

investment.

8. One assumption that must be true in order for a balanced budget

to have a neutral effect on the economy is the assumption that

taxpayers will _____

_____

_____.

9. A balanced budget may have an effect other than a neutral one,
    depending on the following factors:

(1) _____ (2) _____

A Surplus Budget

10. A government is said to have a surplus budget if it _____
    _____ .

11. What are two possible effects of a surplus budget?

    (1) _____

    (2) _____

12. A government may use a surplus budget as a(n) _____
    measure during a period when _____ .

13. A government with a surplus budget will cause the total spending
    in the economy to _____ .

14. When a government has a surplus budget, total spending will be
    _____ than total income and demand will be
    _____ than supply.

A Deficit Budget

15. A government is said to have a deficit budget if it _____
    _____ .

16. What are two possible effects of a deficit budget?

    (1) _____

    (2) _____

17. The taxes paid reduce the spending of individuals and businesses,
    causing contracting effects on _____ and _____,
    but the _____ effects of government
    spending more than offset these contracting effects.

18. When a government has a deficit budget, total spending will

    _____ total income, and demand will _____ the supply

    of goods and services available.

19. If an economy is at less than full employment, a deficit budget

    will _____.

    If an economy is at full employment, a deficit budget will

    _____.

20. Effects of government spending on the circular flow of economic
    activity are listed in the numbered columns below. In the blank
    beside each numbered effect, write the letter identifying the
    type of budget that would produce this effect.

                    a. Surplus budget
                    b. Deficit budget
                    c. Balanced budget

    _____ (1) Neutral effect on economic
              activity and the price level

    _____ (2) Decrease the level of economic
              activity

    _____ (3) Increase the price level

    _____ (4) Decrease the price level

    _____ (5) Increase the level of economic
              activity

III. INFLATION

Definition and Types of Inflation

1. Inflation is a(n) _____ increase in the _____.

2. List the four types of inflation.

    (1) _____   (3) _____

    (2) _____   (4) _____

3. Demand-pull inflation, also known as _____

   inflation, occurs when _____

   _____

   _____.

4. Why is demand-pull inflation more likely to occur in a fully
   employed economy than in an economy at less than full employment?

   _____

   _____

5. In demand-pull inflation, prices are forced upward by _____

   _____

   _____.

6. List five possible causes of the excess spending in demand-pull
   inflation.

   (1) _____

   (2) _____

   (3) _____

   (4) _____

   (5) _____

7. Generally, demand-pull inflation results when the _____

   _____ or _____

   increase faster than _____.

8. Cost-push inflation may occur in either a(n) _____

   or _____ economy.

9. Cost-push inflation may begin with either _____

_____, _____, or _____

_____. An increase in any one of these

three is likely to trigger an increase in one or both of the

other two, which will cause the first to be increased again, and

so on. The name for this continuing increase is the _____

_____.

10. What two factors in recent decades have further intensified
    cost-push inflation?

    (1) _____

    (2) _____

11. Structural inflation, which can occur with _____

    in the economy, arises when _____

    _____

    _____.

12. Two assumptions are part of the concept of structural
    inflation.

    (1) There is a certain amount of _____ and

    _____ among the factors of production, and

    (2) Wages and prices tend to have downward rigidity and upward

    _____ as a result of _____ and

    labor union pressures.

13. In structural inflation, a sudden increase in the demand for the

    products of one industry causes prices in that industry to

    _____ as a result of _____.

59

Then, the expanding industry and industries which have
experienced a decrease in demand compete for the factors of
production, causing increases in wages and prices in all
industries as a result of _____ inflation.

14. Social inflation results from the increasing demand for more
_____, such as

(1) _____   (4) _____

(2) _____   (5) _____

(3) _____   (6) _____

15. Social inflation is also encouraged by the rising cost to private
enterprise originating from _____,
such as the following:

(1) _____   (4) _____

(2) _____   (5) _____

(3) _____

16. Give two examples of other governmental forces which add to price
pressures.

(1) _____

(2) _____

17. At times of full employment, social inflation adds to _____
_____ inflationary pressures. At times of less
than full employment, social inflation can augment _____
or _____ inflationary pressures.

18. One answer to each type of inflation is _____

_____.

19. In demand-pull inflation, if _____

_____,

the inflationary pressure will be removed. On the other hand,

demand for goods and services can be decreased by _____

_____ or _____.

20. Cost-push and structural inflation can be modified if _____

are kept in line with _____.

21. Social inflation can be limited in the following ways:

(1) _____

_____

(2) _____

_____

Stagflation

22. Stagflation is the coexistence of _____ and

_____.

23. Stagflation was heralded by a price level that continued to rise

in spite of a(n) _____ in the economy and a

decrease in _____ associated with the recession

of 1970.

24. What are three major problems of the economies of Canada and the United States?

    (1) _____

    (2) _____

    (3) _____

25. The following statements present some of the difficulties encountered in attempts to alleviate these problems.

    • It is difficult to impose _____ measures

    because they are politically and socially unpopular. List four

    such measures:

    (1) _____ (3) _____

    (2) _____ (4) _____

    • Many of the measures designed to slow down inflation aggravate

    _____.

    • Measures designed to expand the economy and_____

    often exert inflationary pressures on the _____.

SELECTED ANSWERS TO WORKING OUTLINE

I.   CIRCULAR FLOW DEMONSTRATED

A Contracting Economy

17. (A) 10,000; (B) 100,000/90,000/80,000/10,000; (C) 20

18. Units Produced = 100,000
     Inventory Units = 10,000
     Wages, Rent, Interest, Profit (Productive Services Rendered) =
      $200,000
     Money Income = $200,000
     Consumption = $140,000
     Savings = $60,000
     Investment = $40,000
     Delivery of Goods and Services (Demand for Goods and Services) =
      $180,000

An Expanding Economy

24. Units Produced = 100,000
    Wages, Rent, Interest, Profit (Productive Services Rendered) =
      $200,000
    Money Income = $200,000
    Consumption = $140,000
    Savings = $60,000
    Investment = $80,000
    Delivery of Goods and Services (Demand for Goods and Services) =
      $220,000

TERMINOLOGY AND CONCEPTS INTRODUCED

circular flow of economic activity--_____

_____

investment--_____

_____

recession--_____

_____

equilibrium--_____

_____

balanced budget--_____

_____

surplus budget--_____

_____

deficit budget--_____

_____

inflation--_____

_____

demand-pull (excess demand) inflation--_____

_____

cost-push inflation-- _____

_____

wage-price spiral-- _____

_____

administered pricing-- _____

_____

structural inflation-- _____

_____

social inflation-- _____

_____

stagflation-- _____

_____

SAMPLE OBJECTIVE QUESTIONS

1. An economy is said to be contracting when the level of economic
    activity is decreasing. A contracting economy is characterized by an
    accumulation of unsold goods and/or

    (1) an increase in investment
    (2) a decrease in savings
    (3) a decrease in prices
    (4) an increase in spending

2. According to the history of the circular flow of economic activity,
    when an economy is at less than full employment and investment exceeds
    savings, it can be expected that

    A. Total spending will exceed total income
    B. Supply will be greater than demand
    C. There will be an increase in the level of economic activity
    D. Prices will decline

        (1) All of these
        (2) A, B and C only
        (3) A and C only
        (4) B and D only
        (5) C and D only

64

3. Structural inflation is said to result when

    (1) an increase in workers' wages forces up the prices of consumer goods
    (2) demand shifts to the products of one industry which is operating near its capacity and away from those of other industries
    (3) the prices of consumer goods continue to rise in a recessionary period
    (4) the overall demand for goods and services exceeds the supply

ANALYSIS OF SAMPLE OBJECTIVE QUESTIONS

1. Choice (3) is the correct answer. In a contracting economy, savings exceed investment. Therefore, an economy that is characterized by an increase in investment (1) or a decrease in savings (2) would not be a contracting economy. Furthermore, since an increase in spending (4) would cause a decrease in savings, contracting economies do not exhibit increased consumption.

2. Choice (3) is the correct answer. Statements A and C are true. Statement B is incorrect because, when investment exceeds savings, demand exceeds supply, at least in the short run; eventually, supply may increase to meet demand, but supply will not exceed demand as long as investment exceeds savings. Under the circumstances described in the question, prices will not decline, so statement D is false. If the economy were at full employment, it could be expected that competition for scarce factors of production would cause prices to increase.

3. The correct answer is choice (2). Choice (1) is an example of cost-push inflation. Choice (3) describes stagflation. Demand-pull inflation is described in choice (4).

REVIEW QUESTIONS

1. How does the reduced productivity that can occur in a business following inventory accumulation affect the other factors of production?

2. Assume that total planned I exceeds total planned S. How does the level of employment in the economy determine whether there is an increase in the level of economic activity or an increase in the price level?

3. Contrast the effects of a surplus budget with those of a deficit budget.

4. For each type of inflation, state whether it is likely to occur (a) only during times of full employment, (b) only during times of less than full employment, or (c) during times of either full employment or less than full employment.

5. What is administered pricing, and what effect can it have on the economy?

6. The circular flow of economic activity model is crucial to an understanding of this chapter. The model in Figure 4-3 contains all of the elements that were presented in this chapter, but none of them have been labeled. Complete Figure 4-3 by identifying each element present.

Figure 4-3

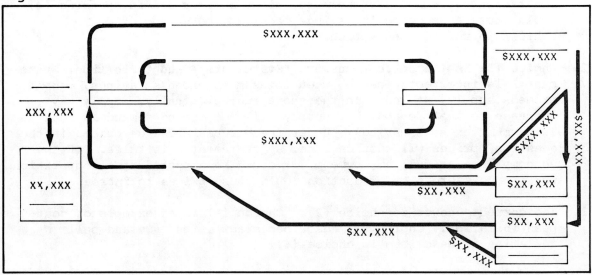

5

Price Determination: The Role of Supply and Demand

OBJECTIVES

In this chapter, you will study supply and demand schedules and will learn the importance of both demand and supply in the pricing of goods. You will discover the impact of changes in demand or supply. The chapter concludes with a discussion of elasticity of demand. Upon completion of this chapter, you should be able to

- Differentiate between the two levels of demand and also between the two levels of supply

- Interpret market demand schedules and market supply schedules

- Distinguish between a movement along a demand or supply curve and a shift in demand or supply

- Explain the consequences of a price higher or lower than the equilibrium price

- Describe the two methods of measuring price elasticity of demand

- Discuss the impact of various factors on price elasticity of demand

WORKING OUTLINE

Introduction

1. In a free enterprise system, a market is established in which the

   final price of a good or service is determined on the basis of

   _____ to the producer and _____

   to the buyer.

I.   THE MARKET MECHANISM

1. Changes in either demand or supply bring about _____
   _____, or _____
   _____, or both.

2. Sometimes, consumer demand is made known to the producers through
   _____. Other times, suppliers try
   to anticipate the demands of consumers and supply the good before
   there is a strong reflection of demand.

3. What are some of the evidences that the market mechanism does not
   work perfectly? _____
   _____
   _____

4. Define derived demand. _____
   _____
   _____

II.   DEMAND

1. What are the two levels of demand?
   (1) _____ (2) _____

Individual Demand

2. Individual demand implies a(n) _____ plus some
   _____.

3. Individual demand signifies the quantity of a good that an
   individual stands ready to buy at _____ at
   _____.

4. The usefulness of a good to an individual at a particular time depends on upon the following two factors:

   (1) _____

   (2) _____

5. Also, the _____ of a commodity will usually

   affect the quantity that an individual will buy at a given time.

Market Demand

6. Market demand (demand) is defined as a schedule of _____

   _____

   _____ .

7. Why is it difficult to construct in advance an accurate demand

   schedule for a specific commodity? _____

   _____

   _____

8. At a given time, consumers will usually buy more units of a good at a low price than they will at a high price for the following three reasons:

   (1) _____

   _____

   _____

   (2) _____

   _____

   _____

   (3) _____

   _____

   _____

9. The quantity of a good that consumers will buy tends to

_____ with the price. However, the variation

in the amount sold is not always _____ to

the change in price.

A Market Demand Schedule

10. The relationship between demand and price can be illustrated as a demand curve on a double-axis graph.

11. Figure 5-1 illustrates the demand curve on Friday at 3 p.m. for shares of Tomasina, Inc., traded on the New York Stock Exchange.

Figure 5-1   Demand Curve for Tomasina Stock

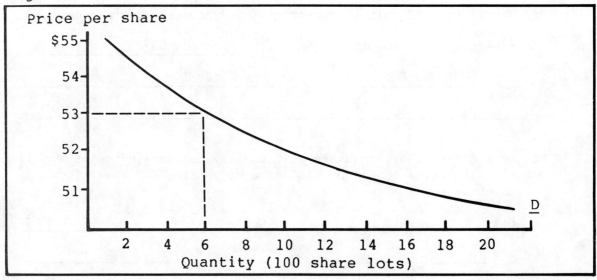

Based on this graph, complete the following statements about the number of shares that investors would purchase at different prices: **(A)**

a. If the price is $54.50 per share, investors will buy _____

lots of 100 shares each.

b. If the price falls to $_____ per share, the investors
    will buy 16 lots.

12. What is an inferior good? _____

_____

Describe the demand curve of an inferior good. _____

_____

Changes in Demand

13. If the price per share of Tomasina stock (see Figure 5-1) dropped
     from $54.50 to $53 and the quantity purchased rose from two lots
     to six lots, this would not represent a change in demand, but
     a(n) _____ along the demand curve, known as a
     change in the _____.

14. A change in demand (a(n) _____ in demand) would result in
     a new demand schedule.

15. An increase in demand means that _____
     _____ will be bought at _____. If a
     second demand curve, $\underline{D}_1$, showing increased demand for Tomasina
     stock, were added to Figure 5-1, it would lie to the _____ of
     $\underline{D}$.

16. A decrease in demand means that _____
     will be bought at _____. If a third
     demand curve, $\underline{D}_2$, showing decreased demand for Tomasina stock,
     were added to Figure 5-1, it would lie to the _____ of $\underline{D}$.

71

17. List five possible causes for a change in demand.

(1) _____

(2) _____

(3) _____

(4) _____

(5) _____

Quantity Sold as a Function of Price

18. The equation expressing the quantity sold as a function of price

is _____ .

19. The equation expressing the quantity sold as a function of all
the factors that influence the quantity sold is

$\underline{q} = \underline{f}\ (\underline{p},\ \underline{DI},\ \underline{p}_x,\ \underline{a}, \ldots)$ where

$\underline{p}$ is the _____ ,

$\underline{DI}$ is the _____ ,

$\underline{p}_x$ is the _____ , and

$\underline{a}$ is the _____ .

III. SUPPLY

Individual Supply

1. The individual supply of a good that is offered on a market

signifies the _____

_____ .

2. To determine the total supply that any individual might offer to

sell, it would be necessary to know _____

_____ .

Market Supply

3. What is the market supply of a good? _____

   _____

   _____

4. A schedule representing the market supply of a good would contain

   all of the _____ that

   all _____ would sell at _____.

A Market Supply Schedule

5. Market supply schedules can be illustrated on a graph similar to

   the graph used to illustrate market demand schedules. A supply

   curve is a line indicating the _____

   _____

   _____.

6. The supply curve rises from _____ to _____.

7. Figure 5-2 illustrates the supply curve on Friday at 3 p.m. for
   shares of Tomasina, Inc.

   Based on this graph, complete the following statements about the
   number of shares that investors would sell at different prices:
   (A)

   a. If the price is $51.50 per share, investors will sell _____

      lots of 100 shares each.

   b. If the price rises to $_____ per share, investors will sell

      20 lots.

Figure 5-2   Supply Curve for Tomasina Stock

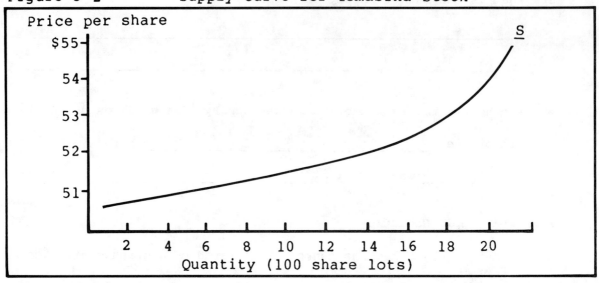

Changes in Supply

8. The supply offered usually tends to _____

    with price, which means that a higher price usually results

    in _____ offered for sale.

9. When price changes and a greater or lesser amount is offered for

    sale, there is not a(n) _____, but

    merely a _____ along the supply curve.

10. A change in supply means that _____

    will be offered for sale _____.

11. An increase in supply means that _____

    will be offered at each price. If a second supply curve, S_1,

    showing an increased supply of Tomasina stock, were added to

    Figure 5-2, it would lie to the _____ of S.

12. A decrease in supply means that_____ will

be offered at each price. If a third supply curve, S_2, showing

a decreased supply of Tomasina stock, were added to Figure 5-2,

it would lie to the _____ of S.

13. The total quantity that will be offered for sale is limited by
the following factors:

(1) _____

_____

(2) _____

_____

14. In the long run, the supply of reproducible goods is conditioned

by _____ and by

_____.

IV.   HOW DEMAND AND SUPPLY DETERMINE PRICE

1. The price of a good will be determined at the point at which the

_____ equals the _____.

This price is known as the _____.

2. Figure 5-3 combines the demand and supply curves for shares of
Tomasina, Inc., from Figures 5-1 and 5-2.

According to this graph, the _____ is

approximately $51.50 per share, and, at that price, approximately

12-1/$_2$ lots of 100 shares each will be sold.

Figure 5-3   Demand and Supply for Tomasina Stock

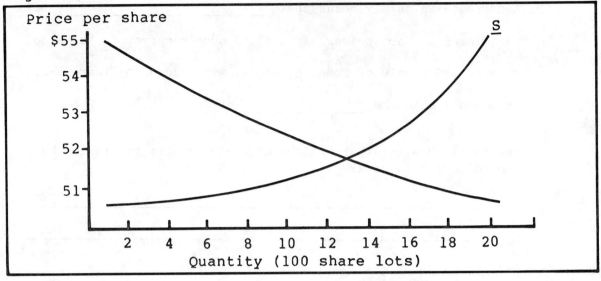

3. If the situation represented in Figure 5-3 is an example of pure

    competition, then no single transaction can affect the _____.

    ● No investor need pay more than, or can pay less than, $51.50 to
      acquire a share of Tomasina stock.

    ● No investor need accept less than, or can demand more than,
      $51.50 to sell a share of Tomasina stock.

4. Under the conditions of supply and demand shown in Figure 5-3, if

    the price per share of Tomasina stock were anything other than

    $51.50, there would be either a shortage--if the price were

    _____ than $51.50, or a surplus--if the price were

    _____ than $51.50.

5. In a free market, although there may be a surplus or a shortage

    of a good in the short run, no price other than the _____

    _____ can prevail.

6. To set the price at other than _____ , the market

will _____ or the forces of

supply and demand _____ . Give

three examples of such price fixing.

(1) _____

(2) _____

(3) _____

7. The following statements summarize the impact of a new relationship between supply and demand.

● If demand increases while supply remains unchanged the price

will _____ and the quantity sold will _____ .

● If demand decreases while supply remains unchanged, the price

will _____ and the quantity sold will _____ .

● If supply increases while demand remains unchanged, the price

will _____ and the quantity sold will _____ .

● If supply decreases while demand remains unchanged, the price

will _____ and the quantity sold will _____ .

V. ELASTICITY OF DEMAND

1. Price elasticity of demand is a measure of _____

_____ .

Measuring Price Elasticity of Demand

2. Elasticity can be measured in the following ways:

(1) _____ (2) _____

3. The formula method measures the relative change in _____

compared to the relative change in _____ .

77

4. The formula for computing pricing elasticity is

$$\text{Price Elasticity} = \frac{(\underline{\hspace{3cm}})}{(\underline{\hspace{3cm}})}$$

5. If the percentage changes are computed using the original price and quantity as bases, the measure of elasticity will be different, depending on whether the price is being _____ or _____. However, if the percentage changes are calculated using an average price base and average quantity base, the percentage change will be _____ whether moving up or down on the price axis.

6. A coefficient of elasticity of 1.0 is known as _____ _____. With a 1.0 coefficient of elasticity, a given change in price will bring about a(n) _____ change in the quantity sold.

7. Unitary elasticity is the point of demarcation between _____ and _____ demand.

8. An elastic demand will have a value _____ than 1.0, indicating that the quantity demanded will change in _____ proportion to the change in price.

9. An inelastic demand will have a value _____ than 1.0, indicating that a change in price will bring about a(n) _____ than proportional change in the quantity sold.

10. The _____ method of measuring

    elasticity is less exact than the formula method, but it tells

    more directly what happens to _____,

    and it shows more clearly the important significance of _____

    _____.

11. According to the total revenue method, if _____

    changes and total revenue _____, unitary elasticity

    of demand exists.

    ● The _____ in revenue resulting from a lower price

       is offset by the increased revenue resulting from a(n) _____

       in sales.

    ● Correspondingly, the increase in revenue resulting from a(n)

       _____ price is offset by the _____

       in revenue resulting from a decrease in sales.

12. According to the total revenue method, if _____ changes

    and total revenue moves in the _____

    _____, demand is elastic.

    ● If prices are lowered, the _____ in revenue from a

       lower price is more than offset by the _____

       revenue from an increase in sales.

    ● If prices are raised, the _____ in revenue from a

       higher price is more than offset by the decreased revenue from

       a(n) _____ in sales.

13. According to the total revenue method, if _____ changes and total revenue moves in the _____ _____, demand is inelastic.

    ● If prices are lowered, the increased revenue resulting from _____ sales is insufficient to make up for the _____ in revenue resulting from the lower price.

    ● If prices are raised, the increased revenue resulting from the higher price is insufficient to make up for the _____ in revenue resulting from lower sales.

14. The measure of elasticity can be applied to supply also.

    ● If a given percentage change in the price of a good results in a(n) _____ percentage change in the quantity supplied, the supply is elastic.

    ● If the percentage change in price results in a(n) _____ percentage change in the quantity offered, the supply is in-elastic.

    ● If the percentage change in price results in a proportionate change in the quantity offered for sale, _____ exists.

Characteristics and Range of Price Elasticity

15. List two difficulties encountered in constructing an empirical demand curve and calculating the elasticity of demand for a product.

    (1) _____

    _____

(2) _____

_____

_____

16. Cite four characteristics of a product or service that help
determine its degree of price elasticity.

(1) _____ (3) _____

(2) _____ (4) _____

17. Perfect elasticity, depicted as a straight _____ line,

indicates that _____

_____.

18. Perfect inelasticity, represented by a straight _____

line, indicates that _____

_____.

19. On any straight-line, slanted demand schedule, there will be

certain areas that are _____, others that are _____,

and--at some spot--the schedule may measure _____

_____.

20. For a demand schedule to possess unitary elasticity throughout,

it would have to be represented by a(n) _____

_____. Then, changes in _____

and _____ would be proportional throughout

the curve.

21. The quantity demanded of a good is affected not only by its

    price, but also by _____.

    This relationship is referred to as _____

    _____.

22. Define the following terms.

    ● substitute good--_____

    _____

    ● complementary good--_____

    _____

23. The quantity demanded for a given good is also affected by the

    _____ of potential consumers.

    ● Although the <u>total</u> demand for goods rises as the level of

      income rises, the demand for <u>each</u> good does not necessarily

      rise _____ with a rise in income.

    ● The relationship between changing income and changes in demand

      for a particular good or service is known as _____

      _____.

SELECTED ANSWERS TO WORKING OUTLINE

II.   DEMAND

A Market Demand Schedule

11. a. If the price is $54.50 per share, investors will buy <u>2</u> lots
         of 100 shares each.

     b. If the prices falls to <u>$51</u> per share, investors will buy 16
         lots.

III. SUPPLY

A Market Supply Schedule

7. a. If the price is $51.50 per share, investors will sell <u>11</u> lots of 100 shares each.

    b. If the price rises to <u>$54</u> per share, investors will sell 20 lots.

TERMINOLOGY AND CONCEPTS INTRODUCED

derived demand--_____

_____

individual demand--_____

_____

market demand (demand)--_____

_____

demand curve--_____

_____

normal goods--_____

_____

inferior goods--_____

_____

individual supply--_____

_____

market supply--_____

_____

supply curve--_____

_____

equilibrium price--_____

_____

price elasticity of demand--_____

_____

unitary elasticity--_____

_____

elastic demand--_____

_____

inelastic demand--_____

_____

perfect elasticity of demand--_____

_____

perfect inelasticity of demand--_____

_____

cross elasticity of demand--_____

_____

substitute good--_____

_____

complementary good--_____

_____

income elasticity of demand--_____

_____

SAMPLE OBJECTIVE QUESTIONS

1. An economist is responsible for illustrating graphically the market demand for a good over an extended time period. The greatest amount of data that the economist can depict with a single market demand curve is the total quantity of a good that purchasers will buy at

    (1) each of several prices at a given time
    (2) a given price at each of several different times
    (3) each of several prices at several different times
    (4) a given price at a given time

2. Assume that, because of problems at the production plant, the supply of a certain home computer has decreased, yet the demand remains unchanged. If all other factors remain unchanged, then it can be expected that this situation will result in

    (1) a decrease in the price and an increase in the quantity sold
    (2) a decrease in both the price and the quantity sold
    (3) an increase in both the price and the quantity sold
    (4) an increase in the price and a decrease in the quantity sold

3. Using the formula method, the price elasticity of demand for an economic good is found by dividing

    (1) change in price by change in quantity
    (2) change in quantity by change in price
    (3) percent of change in price by percent of change in quantity
    (4) percent of change in quantity by percent of change in price

4. The nature of a good influences the price elasicity of demand for the good. The following goods tend to be price inelastic:

    A. Perishable goods
    B. Goods which require small budget expenditures
    C. Luxury goods
    D. Complementary goods
    E. Goods with limited uses

    (1) All of these
    (2) A, B, D and E only
    (3) A, B and D only
    (4) A, C and E only
    (5) B, C and E only

5. A demand curve is a schedule of prices and quantities. A measure of the price elasticity of a product can be obtained from a graph of the product's demand curve. For a given product, a straight horizontal demand curve would depict

   (1) perfect price inelasticity of demand
   (2) unit price elasticity of demand
   (3) perfect price elasticity of demand
   (4) cross elasticity of demand

ANALYSIS OF SAMPLE OBJECTIVE QUESTIONS

1. Choice (1) is the correct answer. A market demand curve only contains data applicable to one point in time, not to several different times (2 and 3). However, a market demand curve does illustrate the quantity demanded at several prices, not at only one price (4).

2. The correct answer is choice (4); choices (1), (2) and (3) are all incorrect. A decrease in supply relative to demand will result in an increase in the price and the sale of a smaller amount of the good.

3. Choice (4) is the correct answer. Choices (1) and (2) are incorrect because the formula method compares the percent of change in quantity and price, not the absolute change. Choice (3) reverses the positions of the numerator and denominator of the expression, and therefore is wrong.

4. The correct answer is choice (2); statements A, B, D, and E all contain examples of goods that tend to be price inelastic. Luxury goods tend to be price elastic. Therefore, statement C is incorrect.

5. The correct answer is choice (3). Choices (1), (2), and (4) are all incorrect. If a good has perfect elasticity of demand, then an infinite amount of the product could be sold without a change in price. The demand curve for such a good would be a straight horizontal line.

REVIEW QUESTIONS

1. Use an example to illustrate the concept of derived demand.

2. What is the significance of a movement along the demand curve? of a shift in the demand curve?

3. It is said that the forces of demand and supply are impersonal. What is the significance of this statement?

4. Explain the process by which an out-of-balance situation characterized by by a shortage of a good is brought into balance at the equilibrium price. Explain the process for resolving situations characterized by a surplus.

5. For a given product, what changes occur in the price and the quantity sold as a result of increased/decreased supply or demand?

6. A certain product normally sells for $25, but local retailers have lowered its price to $15 for a special promotion. According to the supply and demand curves for this product, the quantity sold should increase from 1,200 to 2,000 as a direct result of this sale. What is the coefficient of elasticity for this product? **(A)**

7. If the price of the product described in #6 is lowered from $15 to $13.50, how many additional units should be sold? **(A)**

8. Of what significance is information about price elasticity of demand to sellers? To consumers?

9. List the characteristics of those goods that tend toward elastic demand and of those that tend toward inelastic demand.

10. On the three simplified graphs in Figure 5-4 below, depict (a) perfectly unitary elasticity, (b) perfectly inelastic demand, and (c) perfectly elastic demand.

Figure 5-4   Different Elasticities

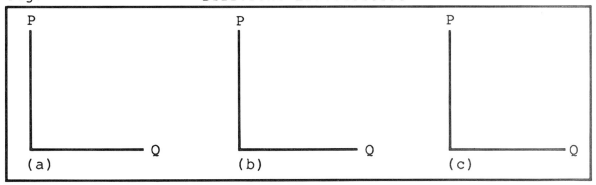

(a)   (b)   (c)

ANSWERS TO SELECTED REVIEW QUESTIONS

6. $\dfrac{(2,000 - 1,200) \div [(1,200 + 2,000) \div 2)]}{(\$25 - \$15) \div [(\$15 + \$25)] \div 2]} = \dfrac{800 \div 1,600}{\$10 \div \$20} = \dfrac{.50}{.50} = 1.0$

7. $\dfrac{\$15 - \$13.50}{\$15} = \dfrac{\$1.50}{\$15} = .10$

    2,000 x .10 = 200 additional units

6
Production, Cost, and Profit

In this chapter, you will study the types of costs incurred in manufacturing a good. You will become acquainted with the law of diminishing returns. You will also see how firms can determine the optimum quantity to produce. Upon completion of this chapter, you should be able to

- Discuss the impact of the law of diminishing returns

- Compute the marginal product, marginal cost, and marginal revenue of a good

- Identify the classifications of the cost of production

- Interpret graphs illustrating the cost of production or the break-even point

- Distinguish between pure profit and nominal profit

- Describe how break-even analysis and marginal analysis can be used to determine a firm's optimum profit situation

WORKING OUTLINE

Introduction

1. In situations of pure competition, there is nothing a firm can do to control its cost per unit of input because _____

_____

_____

_____.

2. List three methods by which a firm can alter its cost per unit of output.

   (1) _____

   (2) _____

   (3) _____

3. A firm's cost of production largely determines the _____

   _____ that it offers on the market and affects _____

   _____.

I. THE PRODUCTION FUNCTION

1. The relationship between _____ and _____

   _____ is called the production function.

2. The production function exhibits certain properties that

   determine the way in which cost varies with _____.

Law of Diminishing Returns

3. The essential function of management in providing a supply of

   goods is to organize land, capital, and labor so that _____

   _____.

4. In every instance where goods are being produced, there is a(n)

   _____ of the factors of production, which is

   determined, in part, by the law of _____

   (law of diminishing productivity).

5. The marginal product (MP) of any input is the _____

   _____.

6. According to the law of diminishing returns (_____

_____), as additional units of a factor

of production are combined with _____ of other

factors, a point will be reached where the _____

resulting from the use of an additional unit of that factor will

not be as large as was the _____ due to the

addition of the preceding unit.

7. Eventually, there is a point at which fixed factors are used to
full capacity, so that the addition of one unit of input results
either in no increase in output or in a decrease in output.

8. The average product (AP) is the _____

_____.

9. The AP, like the _____, increases, reaches a maximum,

and then _____.

10. Any time the MP is _____ than the AP, it causes the AP

to increase; when the MP is _____ than the AP, it

reduces the AP.

11. To pull down the AP, the MP must be _____

_____, not merely _____.

Returns to Scale

12. Under what circumstances would the following returns to scale be
said to exist?

    (1) Constant returns to scale--_____

    _____

90

(2) Decreasing returns to scale-- _____

_____

(3) Increasing returns to scale-- _____

_____

II. COSTS OF PRODUCTION

1. For all practical purposes, the measure of production cost is

   _____.

2. In a capitalistic economy, _____ is considered to

   be a cost of production, along with payments for _____,

   _____, _____, and other items

   directly or indirectly related to production.

Alternative Uses and Opportunity Costs

3. Under a system of private enterprise, a factor of production is
   usually employed for production of a specific good only if

   _____

   _____

   _____.

4. Opportunity cost is that income which _____

   _____

   _____. This

   cost exists whether payment is made in the form of _____

   _____ or not.

Explicit and Imputed Costs

5. Explicit costs are expenditures for production that result from

    _____. These costs are always recognized

    because they are _____

    and are _____.

6. Expenditures that are attributable to _____

    _____ are imputed costs (implicit

    costs). Although imputed costs are often ignored in normal

    accounting procedure, they must be recognized as a part of

    _____ in determining the

    _____.

Classifications of Costs

7. In the left-hand column below are seven common abbreviations for
    various cost classifications. In the space that follows each
    abbreviation, write the term for which that abbreviation stands.

    (1) AFC--_____

    (2) ATC--_____

    (3) AVC--_____

    (4) MC--_____

    (5) TC--_____

    (6) TFC--_____

    (7) TVC--_____

8. Unless the plant capacity is changed, the amount of TFC in a firm

    does not vary with the _____.

9. TFC is frequently referred to as _____.

10. List five types of expenses which can be included in TFC.

    (1) _____

    (2) _____

    (3) _____

    (4) _____

    (5) _____

11. Although TFC remains constant, AFC decreases with _____

    _____. AFC will continue to grow smaller as

    more units are produced, but it will never disappear entirely.

12. List two examples of TVC.

    (1) _____ (2) _____

13. As long as the price of variable factors _____,

    AVC decreases as production increases until the _____

    _____ is reached.

14. The point of lowest AVC corresponds with the point of highest

    _____.

15. As production increases, TC _____, but not

    proportionally.

16. As production increases, ATC usually _____ until

    soon after the point of diminishing returns is reached. Then ATC

    _____ as production increases.

93

17. <u>MC</u> is strongly influenced by the _____

_____ .

18. The shape of any <u>MC</u> curve will depend upon the shape of the

_____ curve.

19. The values of <u>MC</u> _____ , reach a(n) _____ ,

and then _____ thereafter.

20. The point of _____ <u>MC</u> corresponds with the point

of _____ <u>MP</u>, revealing the close, but _____ ,

relationship between <u>MP</u> and <u>MC</u>.

21. The following statements can correctly be made about a graphic
representation of these types of cost values:

(1) <u>AFC</u> will be represented by a curve, continuously _____

_____ in value.

(2) <u>AVC</u> will be a curve _____ , reaching a(n) _____ ,

and then _____ in value.

(3) <u>ATC</u> will drop while both _____ and _____ are falling.

(4) There is a point at which the <u>AVC</u> starts to rise while the

<u>AFC</u> is still _____ . What happens to the

<u>ATC</u> at this point will depend on _____

_____ .

(5) Anytime <u>MC</u> is less than <u>AVC</u> or <u>ATC</u>, it will _____

_____ .

(6) Whenever <u>MC</u> is greater than the <u>AVC</u> or <u>ATC</u>, it will _____

_____ .

94

(7) <u>MC</u> will intersect the _____ and _____ lines at their lowest points.

III. REVENUE AND PROFIT

Revenues

1. _____ (_____) is the revenue per unit sold. From the viewpoint of the seller, it is the _____ _____.

2. Total revenue (<u>TR</u>) is the _____ _____.

3. If <u>TR</u> can be computed as <u>TR</u> = <u>AR</u> x number of units sold, then <u>AR</u> = _____.

4. Marginal revenue (<u>MR</u>) is the _____ that results from _____.

5. <u>MR</u> can be calculated by _____ the increase in total revenue resulting from the use of an additional unit of _____ by the increase in _____.

6. Under perfectly competitive conditions, the values of _____ and _____ will be identical.

Profit

7. Total profit is the difference between _____ and _____.

8. Whether a firm makes a profit, and how much profit it makes,

   depends on the _____

   _____ .

Total Revenue Versus Total Cost

9. By comparing total revenue with total cost over a given range of output, a firm can determine the following:

   (1) _____

   (2) _____

   (3) _____

10. What is a break-even point? _____

    _____

11. The break-even point can be expressed in any of the following three ways:

    (1) _____

    (2) _____

    (3) _____

12. The maximum profit position for a firm will be that level of

    output, or capacity, where _____

    _____ .

13. One advantage of a break-even chart is that cost can be broken

    down into _____ and _____ .

14. The following statements can correct be made about a break-even chart:

    (1) TFC is represented by a(n) _____ line.

(2) TC is represented by a line moving _____.

(3) The difference between TC and TFC represents the _____.

(4) If the price at which each unit sells is constant, the TR

line will move _____ to the _____

at a(n) _____.

(5) The break-even point occurs at the intersection of the _____

line and the _____ line.

Marginal Revenue Versus Marginal Cost

15. Whenever the production and sale of a marginal unit add more to

revenue than to cost, _____ will increase, or

_____ will diminish, whatever the case may be.

16. Profits will decrease, or losses will increase, whatever the case

may be, whenever the production and sale of a marginal unit add

more to _____ than to _____.

17. A firm will profit by increasing its output so long as _____

_____. It will pay to reduce output whenever

_____.

18. In most cases, MR is a(n)_____ or_____

value, and MC is a(n) _____value.

19. A firm reaches its maximum profit position at the point at which

_____.

Minimizing Losses in the Short Run

20. Each of the following terms has a definition that is specific to the study of economics. Give these definitions.

    • Market period--_____

    _____

    • Short run--_____

    _____

    • Long run--_____

    _____

21. If a firm is operating at a loss in the short run, the decision to continue to operate or to shut down will depend on the following relationships:

    (1) _____

    (2) _____

22. In the short run, a firm will benefit from operating at a loss as

    long as it can _____

    _____. If

    the firm cannot _____, however,

    it will be more profitable to shut down in the short run.

23. These considerations can be stated as a mathematical expression:

    If _____ > _____, the firm

    should continue to operate.

24. Whether the firm desires to continue operations in the long run under a loss condition will depend, in part, on the following factors:

    (1) _____   (3) _____

    (2) _____   (4) _____

IV. PURE PROFIT

1. From an economic point of view, profit is a(n) _____ of income over and above all economic costs, both _____ and _____.

2. Profits are _____ in that they are constantly changing in amount.

3. Pure profit (_____ profit) is an amount entre-preneurs receive from the operation of a business. It is their return on the factor of production that they supply--their entrepreneurship. Pure profit excludes any return from the use of the other factors of production utilized in the input mix.

4. Nominal profit is that amount of profit that _____ _____.

5. Nominal profit is measured by _____ _____.

6. Pure profit is any amount over and above _____.

7. Under conditions of _____, profit is a temporary phenomenon.

8. Under a condition of _____ or _____ competition, profits may be larger than they would be under _____.

TERMINOLOGY AND CONCEPTS INTRODUCED

production function--_____

_____

law of diminishing returns (law of diminishing marginal
productivity)--_____

_____

marginal product (MP)--_____

_____

average product (AP)--_____

_____

constant returns to scale--_____

_____

decreasing returns to scale--_____

_____

increasing returns to scale--_____

_____

opportunity cost--_____

_____

explicit costs--_____

_____

imputed (implicit) costs--_____

_____

fixed costs--_____

_____

total fixed cost (TFC)--_____

_____

overhead--_____

_____

average fixed cost (AFC)--_____

_____

variable costs--_____

_____

average variable cost (AVC)--_____

_____

total variable costs (TVC)--_____

_____

total cost (TC)--_____

_____

average total cost (ATC)--_____

_____

marginal cost (MC)--_____

_____

average revenue (AR)--_____

_____

total revenue (TR)--_____

_____

marginal revenue (MR)--_____

_____

break-even point--_____

_____

market period--_____

_____

short run--_____

_____

long run--_____

_____

profit--_____

_____

nominal profit--_____

_____

pure profit--_____

_____

SAMPLE OBJECTIVE QUESTIONS

1. In economics, "the production output per unit of factor input" is the
    definition of

    (1) elasticity of supply
    (2) marginal utility
    (3) the average product
    (4) the marginal product

2. If the plant capacity of a firm remains unchanged, fixed costs per
    unit of production normally will

    (1) remain constant as the output varies
    (2) decrease with an increase in output
    (3) increase with an increase in output
    (4) increase with an increase in variable costs

3. The amount of profit necessary to induce an entrepreneur to stay in
    business is measured by the opportunity cost of the entrepreneur's
    services. The term economists use to refer to this type of profit is

    (1) nominal profit
    (2) pure profit
    (3) inducement profit
    (4) marginal profit

ANALYSIS OF SAMPLE OBJECTIVE QUESTIONS

1. Choice (3) is the correct answer. Choices (1), (2), and (4) are all incorrect. If three units of labor are used to produce nine units of output, then the production output per unit of factor input, or the average product (AP), is three units of output.

2. The correct answer is choice (2). "Fixed costs per unit of production" is another way of saying average fixed costs (AFC). Choice (1) is incorrect because, although total fixed costs (TFC) remain constant as the output varies, AFC changes as the output varies. The larger the number of units of production over which to spread the TFC, the smaller the AFC; therefore, choice (3) is wrong. Choice (4) is wrong because, although total cost (TC) varies with changes in variable costs, variable costs are not considered in the computation of AFC.

3. The correct answer is choice (1), which represents the opportunity cost of the entrepreneur's services. Choice (2) is incorrect because pure profit is defined as profit over and above nominal profit. Choices (3) and (4) are not terms typically used in economics.

REVIEW QUESTIONS

1. In your own words, state the law of diminishing returns (law of diminishing marginal productivity).

2. Explain through example the concept of opportunity cost.

3. Distinguish between explicit costs and imputed (implicit) costs.

4. Why is it appropriate to consider a portion of the salaries a firm pays for executive and supervisory services as fixed expenses?

5. Table 6-1 contains partial data about the production of a certain good. Complete the chart by determining the numbers which should appear in the blanks. **(A)**

Table 6-1

Input	Output	MP $	TC $	MC $	TR $	MR $
5	80	NA	120	NA	180.00	NA
6	94	_____	140	_____	211.50	_____

6. Why are AR and MR identical under perfectly competitive conditions? Why do they differ under other conditions?

7. Of what use is break-even analysis to the management of a firm? What types of cost segmentation can be illustrated on a break-even chart?

8. Assume that a firm has a TFC of $75,000, a TVC of $90,000, and a TR of $100,000. In the short run, should the firm shut down or continue to operate? Would the decision be different if the firm had TR of $80,000? Justify your answer. (A)

ANSWERS TO SELECTED REVIEW QUESTIONS

5. MP = 94 - 80 = 14

$$MC = \frac{\$140 - \$120}{94 - 80} = \frac{\$20}{14} = \$1.43$$

$$MR = \frac{\$211.50 - \$180.00}{94 - 80} = \frac{\$31.50}{14} = \$2.25$$

8. With TR of $100,000, the firm can meet its TVC of $90,000 and have $10,000 to offset a portion of the $75,000 TFC; therefore, the firm should continue its operations in the short run. If TR fell to $80,000, the firm would be unable to pay its TVC of $90,000. Then, since the firm would lose $75,000 if it shut down, but would lose an additional $10,000 ($90,000 - $80,000) if it continued to operate, it should shut down.

7

Pure Competition: A Theoretical Model

OBJECTIVES

In this chapter, you will become familiar with the conditions of pure competition. You will study the short- and long-run changes that can occur in an industry because of the forces of pure competition. Upon completion of this chapter, you should be able to

- Identify the characteristics of pure competition

- Describe how firms determine the quantity of output to produce

- Explain how some firms can make a profit, while others break-even, and still others suffer losses, when all firms sell their goods at the same market price

- Summarize the processes whereby profits or losses are eliminated from an industry under conditions of pure competition

- Discuss the significance of the optimum scale of operations

WORKING OUTLINE

Introduction

1. What are the four basic types of market structure?

   (1) _____ (3) _____

   (2) _____ (4) _____

2. List three characteristics that can be used to distinguish among the different types of markets.

   (1) _____

   (2) _____

   (3) _____

I. CHARACTERISTICS OF PURE COMPETITION

1. Pure competition is considered a(n) _____ set of

   market conditions.

2. Under conditions of pure competition, there are _____

   sellers in the market, all selling _____.

   - List three factors which might normally differentiate the
     products of various sellers which are absent from pure
     competition:

     (1) _____

     (2) _____

     (3) _____

3. All _____ and sellers are informed about markets

   and _____, under pure competition.

   - All consumers know if one seller is offering a better price
     than the others.

   - If one producer discovers a cost-saving advantage, all other
     producers can learn why and how this was achieved.

4. There is free _____ and _____ from the

   market, under conditions of pure competition.

   - Anyone who desires to _____ goods in a

     particular market can do so.

5. In the space to the left of each of the following five conditions, indicate whether that condition would be present or absent under pure competition.

_____(1) Patent rights protection

_____(2) Excessive capital requirements

_____(3) Available factors of production

_____(4) Government regulations

_____(5) Perfectly mobile factors of production

6. Pure competition assumes that no _____

_____ can influence price.

   ● Price is determined by _____ and _____

   _____.

   ● Although no seller will be able to obtain a price greater than

   the _____, the actions of many, or all, firms

   can result in a change in the _____.

7. In comparison with the term <u>pure competition</u>, the term <u>perfect</u>
<u>competition</u> is more _____ and represents

a higher _____.

II. PRICE AND PROFIT IN THE SHORT RUN

1. Under pure competition, each producer faces a(n) _____

_____--which is to say that

the producer's _____ can be sold at the

market-determined price.

2. Profit is equal to (Selling price - _____) x _____

107

3. Each producer will try to produce that number of units whose sale

_____ .

4. If many, or all, producers increase or decrease production, the

_____ will be affected.

This will result in_____ , as long as _____

does not change.

5. Given conditions which cannot be changed in the short run, each

producer will attempt to set output at the point where _____

_____ equals _____ .

Adjustment of Production to Price in the Short Run

6. List two reasons why it is difficult to determine the exact
number of units that a single firm will produce.

(1) _____

(2) _____

7. It is assumed that an entrepreneur will undertake to produce that

amount which will _____ or _____

_____ .

8. What that volume of production will be depends on the firm's

_____ .

9. The difference between $\underline{AR}$ (or price) and $\underline{ATC}$ represents profit

per unit. Profit per unit multiplied by the output measures

_____ .

10. The point where $\underline{MC} = \underline{MR}$ is called the equilibrium point because

_____

_____

_____.

 • If $\underline{MC} < \underline{MR}$, an _____ of output will increase profit.

 • If $\underline{MC} > \underline{MR}$, a _____ of output will increase profit.

 • If $\underline{MC} = \underline{MR}$, total profit is at the maximum.

11. If $\underline{MC}$ and $\underline{MR}$ do not coincide exactly for the production of a whole unit of output, then it would be most profitable to _____

_____.

* * * * * *

Statements 12 through 15 relate to Figure 7-1 below which illustrates four different cost and revenue relationships.

Figure 7-1   Cost and Revenue Curves

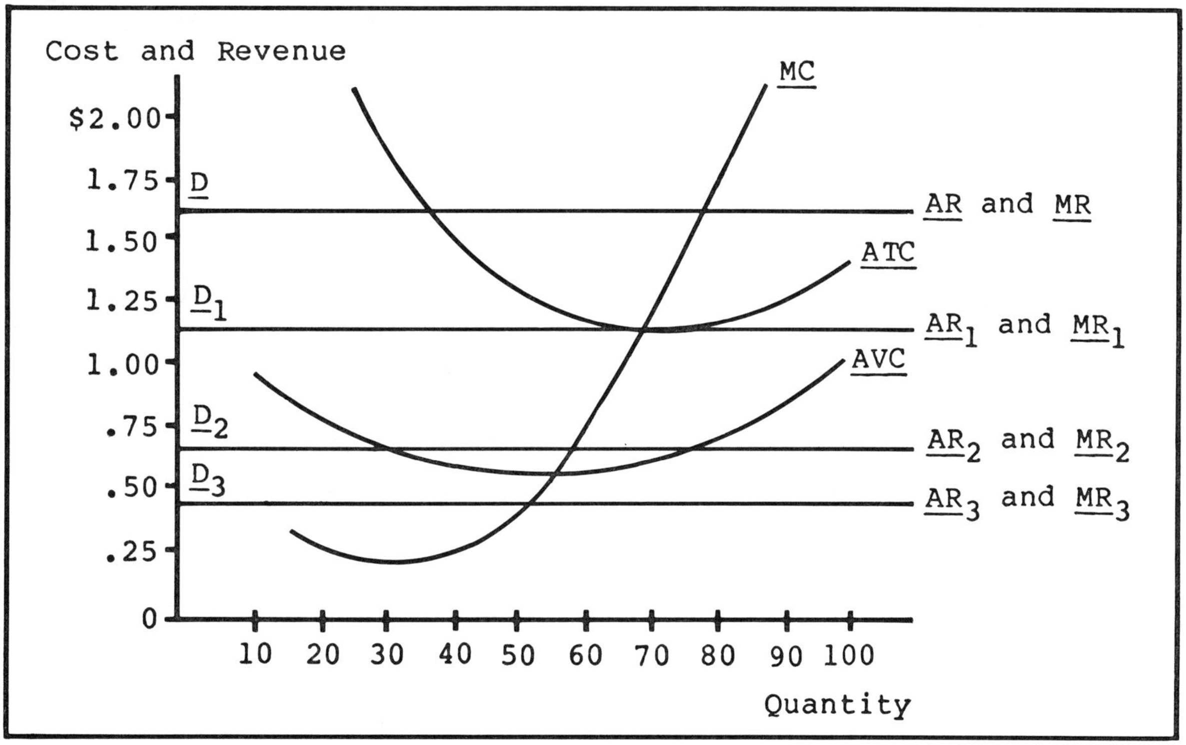

109

12. In the first relationship, where revenue is represented by $\underline{AR}$ and $\underline{MR}$, the firm will maximize profit if it produces approximately

_____ units of output. **(A)**

13. If the price per unit falls to approximately \$1.13, as in $\underline{AR}_1$ and $\underline{MR}_1$, then the most the producer can hope for is to break even.

(1) By producing 70 units, $\underline{AR}$ will be just equal to_____ . **(A)**

(2) The firm will lose money if it produces more than 70 units, because _____ and _____ will rise above $\underline{AR}_1$ and $\underline{MR}_1$. **(A)**

(3) The firm will lose money if it produces less than 70 units, because _____ will be greater than $\underline{AR}_1$. **(A)**

14. If the price per unit falls below approximately \$1.13, as in $\underline{AR}_2$ and $\underline{AR}_3$, the producer cannot _____ and must seek the point at which the loss can be minimized. **(A)**

(1) At $\underline{AR}_2$ and $\underline{MR}_2$, the firm should produce approximately _____ units. **(A)**

(2) At $\underline{AR}_3$ and $\underline{MR}_3$, the firm can minimize losses from operation if it produces approximately _____ units. **(A)**

15. At the equilibrium level for $\underline{AR}_2$ and $\underline{MR}_2$, the firm should continue to operate in the short run because $\underline{AR}$ _____ AVC. However, at the equilibrium level for $\underline{AR}_3$ and $\underline{MR}_3$, the firm should shut down in the short run because $\underline{AR}$ _____ AVC. **(A)**

******

Short-Run Equilibrium Price

16. The price which results from _____

    _____ over a short period is known as the

    competitive short-run equilibrium price.

17. Define the following terms:

    (1) Submarginal producers--_____

    (2) Supramarginal producers--_____

18. The short-run equilibrium price is not a(n) _____ price.

19. In the left-hand column below are three circumstances which
    contribute to the instability of the short-run equilibrium price.
    In the blank beside each circumstance, write the letter
    identifying the market reaction in the right-hand column that
    would accompany that circumstance.

    __(1) Submarginal producers improve   a. Market supply increases,
         their efficiency   causing price to drop

    __(2) Submarginal producers exit   b. Market supply decreases,
         from the market   causing price to rise

    __(3) Supramarginal producers attract
         new producers into the market

III. PRICE AND PROFIT IN THE LONG RUN

1. Under conditions of pure competition, economic profits are
   residual, dynamic, and temporary. Explain why each of these
   terms is an appropriate modifier for economic profits.

   ● Residual--_____

   ● Dynamic--_____

   ● Temporary--_____

Profit Differentiation Among Firms

2. Although, under pure competition, all firms pay an identical price for _____ and receive a uniform _____ for output, it is still possible for profits among firms to differ.

3. Explain how some producers can have a lower per unit cost of output. _____

_____

_____

4. What is a marginal producer? _____

_____.

5. A change in the market price can affect the _____ of each firm.

6. A change in the per unit cost of inputs can also affect the profit of each firm by altering its _____

_____.

7. Under conditions of pure competition, it is assumed that sub-marginal firms will reorganize their productive factors to _____ or will exit from the market.

How Profits Disappear

8. Under pure competition, competitive forces tend to _____

_____.

9. The disappearance of profits is primarily due to the freedom of firms to _____ and _____ the industry.

10. If _____ is being made by _____, outsiders can gather information on how to produce and share in the profits being made.

11. The entry of many new producers into the market causes a(n) _____ in the market supply, resulting in a(n) _____ in the market price. This process continues until market price equals the _____ _____ and _____ is eliminated.

12. If the market price is below cost, causing firms to suffer losses, some firms will _____. This action will result in a(n) _____ in market supply and a(n) _____ in price so that losses disappear in the industry.

13. Under conditions of pure competition, if there is no pure profit in an industry, then all of the firms are in equilibrium because _____ _____, and the industry itself is in equilibrium because _____ _____.

14. The movement from a short-run profit position to a long-run, no-pure-profit equilibrium can be caused by adjustments in the

    _____ or _____.

15. A long-run, no-pure-profit equilibrium can also be brought about by a(n) _____ on the _____.

    ● As new firms enter the industry, their combined demand for

       _____ can increase the total demand, raising

       the market price of _____ and the _____ curve for

       individual firms, causing a(n) _____ in profit.

The Long-Run Cost Curve

16. Under pure competition, or highly competitive conditions, the

    consumer obtains a good or service in the long run at _____

    _____.

17. Because of competition, price, in the long run, is equal to

    _____, or the _____

    point on the _____ curve.

18. If cost advantages arising from large size allow some firms to make a profit, other firms will enlarge their operations.

    ● This action will cause the total supply in the market to

       _____, forcing market price _____.

    ● Some firms will continue to try to benefit from enlarging their

       scale of operations until a point of _____

       is reached on the scale of operations.

114

19. The _____ is that point
at which a producer has obtained all possible cost advantages
arising from size.

20. By joining short-run ATC curves, we can develop a(n) _____
_____.

21. At any scale of operations up to the _____, it is
said that economics of scale exist because _____
_____.

22. Beyond the optimum scale of operations, _____
come into existence, causing the long-run ATC to _____.

SELECTED ANSWERS TO WORKING OUTLINE

II. PRICE AND PROFIT IN THE SHORT RUN

Adjustment of Production to Price in the Short Run

12. 80

13. (1) ATC
    (2) ATC, MC
    (3) ATC

14. hope to make a profit

    (1) 60
    (2) 50

15. >, <

TERMINOLOGY AND CONCEPTS INTRODUCED

pure competition--_____

_____

perfect competition--_____

_____

short-run equilibrium price--_____

_____

submarginal producers--_____

_____

supramarginal producers--_____

_____

marginal producers--_____

_____

optimum scale of operations--_____

_____

economies of scale--_____

_____

diseconomies of scale--_____

_____

SAMPLE OBJECTIVE QUESTIONS

1. Pure competition implies an ideal set of market conditions in which
    there would be numerous sellers in the market, all selling identical
    products, and in which

    (1) only advertising differentiates among the products of the
        various sellers
    (2) each producer faces a perfectly elastic demand curve
    (3) any individual or seller can influence price
    (4) there is limited entry into and exit from the market

2. There are some situations in which a firm cannot make a profit and must choose either to operate at a loss in the short run or to shut down operations. Assume that, in an industry operating under conditions of pure competition, a firm faces such a decision. It will be less costly for the firm to shut down operations only if at the equilibrium level of production its

   (1) average variable cost is less than its average revenue
   (2) marginal revenue is less than its marginal cost
   (3) marginal product is less than its average total cost
   (4) average revenue is less than its average variable cost

3. From an economic point of view, profit is a residual of the income over the costs that result from the operation of a business. The following statements can correctly be made about profit under market conditions of pure competition:

   A. At any given market price, it is possible to have some firms making a profit, others breaking even, and still others suffering a loss
   B. In the long run, if losses are generally being suffered, market forces tend to bring about adjustments that can cause profit to appear
   C. In the long run, market forces act to eliminate or reduce pure profit
   D. Profit is dynamic in that it is constantly changing in amount

      (1) All of these
      (2) A, B and D only
      (3) A, C and D only
      (4) B, C and D only
      (5) B and C only

ANALYSIS OF SAMPLE OBJECTIVE QUESTIONS

1. Choice (2) is the correct answer. Choice (1) is incorrect because there is no advertising under conditions of pure competition. With pure competition, no individual seller or consumer can influence price, so choice (3) is wrong. Under conditions of pure competition, there is free entry into and exit from the market, so choice (4) is a false statement.

2. The correct answer is choice (4); choices (1), (2), and (3) are all incorrect. If a firm cannot make a profit at any level of production, it must determine whether it can at least recover its variable costs. If its average variable costs (AVC) are equal to or less (1) than its average revenue (AR), it can recover its variable costs and possibly make a contribution to its overhead. Only if its AR is less than its ATC should the firm shut down. Choice (2) is nonsensical because, at the equilibrium level of production, marginal revenue (MR) equals marginal cost (MC). Choice (3) is incorrect because the firm must evaluate its average revenue rather than its marginal product to see if it can cover its ATC.

3. Choice (1) is the correct answer. Statements A, B, C, and D are all true statements about profit under conditions of pure competition.

REVIEW QUESTIONS

1. What is the rationale for studying pure competition before any of the other types of market structure?

2. Specifically, how does perfect competition differ from pure competition?

3. Explain the importance to an individual firm of the equilibrium point in terms of units of output.

4. From what two angles do the competitive forces in the economy work to eliminate profits in the long run?

8

Imperfect Competition: The World of Reality

OBJECTIVES

In this chapter, you will study the market conditions known as monopoly, competitive monopoly, and oligopoly. You will examine how prices are determined in each type of market and you will discover why a purely competitive market is best for consumers. You will become familiar with some of the more important pieces of antitrust legislation in the United States and Canada. Upon completion of this chapter, you should be able to

- Distinguish among conditions of monopoly, monopolistic competition, and oligopoly

- Identify the sources of monopoly

- Explain why a monopolist cannot arbitrarily set a high price and expect to receive a large profit

- Describe the impact of differentiated products on the pricing of products in a monopolistic competition

- Discuss the factors which promote price rigidity in an oligopoly

- Identify the varying degrees of competition among consumers

- Distinguish among the major antitrust laws

WORKING OUTLINE

I.   MONOPOLY

1. At the other end of the competitive scale from _____

    is pure monopoly.

2. Pure monopoly is a market condition in which there is only _____

_____

and there are no _____

_____.

3. Pure monopoly, like pure competition, is more of a(n) _____

than a reality.

4. Even if a firm were a pure monopolist in the sale of a particular

good or service, it could claim to be in competition with other

firms for the acquisition of _____.

5. In the economies of Canada and the United States, pure monopoly

is nonexistent except for _____

_____.

The Characteristics of Monopoly

6. The major characteristic of monopoly is the _____

_____

_____.

7. The individual supply of the monopolist is identical to _____

_____, and the total market demand is the

demand for the monopolist's good or service.

8. Any time the monopolist increases or decreases supply, this

increase or decrease will _____.

9. Within limits, the monopolist can _____

to attain the most favorable market price.

120

10. Does the monopolist have absolute control over the market price? _____ Explain your answer. _____

_____

Sources of Monopoly

11. The essence of obtaining and maintaining a monopoly is the _____

_____

_____.

12. List three barriers that can block the entry of a new firm into an industry.

    (1) _____

    (2) _____

    (3) _____

13. In some industries, it is uneconomical for firms to operate

    competitively because, if many firms were present in the market,

    no one firm could produce enough to take advantage of the

    _____ associated with _____

    _____. In such industries,

    the largest firms are not pure monopolies, but tend to have

    _____.

14. The existence of natural monopolies for such goods and services as public utilities prevents the confusion, waste, and inconvenience that would result if numerous firms competed.

    ● In such industries, if one or two firms can adequately supply

      all the service needed, it is desirable to _____

      _____ within a given

      territory.

121

● Under these circumstances government must regulate services and prices. What is the customary means of providing such regulation? _____

_____

_____

15. A firm can retain a monopoly position through the ownership or control of _____. Often, however, there is a close substitute for a particular _____ _____.

16. A patent gives the holder the exclusive right _____ _____ for a set number of years (_____ in both Canada and the United States).

17. The control of patents is an important source of _____ _____ for some large corporations.

18. Briefly describe three ways in which a corporation could use patents and/or patent laws to stifle competition.

(1) _____

_____

(2) _____

_____

(3) _____

_____

19. A firm may eliminate its rivals or block the entry of new firms

through the use of _____

_____ .

20. List five unfair (and sometimes illegal) tactics which some firms
have employed to drive out competition.

(1) _____

(2) _____

(3) _____

(4) _____

(5) _____

II. PURE MONOPOLY PRICE

1. The monopolist does not always exercise its power to obtain the

_____ for what is sold.

2. Describe the two alternative conditions under which pure monopoly
can occur.

(1) _____

_____

(2) _____

_____

Determination of Monopoly Price

3. Within limits, a monopolist can _____

at virtually any level.

4. The price will be _____ for all consumers and can

    be set by the seller at that point which _____

    _____. The

    location of this point depends upon the following two factors:

    (1) _____ (2) _____

5. The demand curve for the monopolist's product slopes _____

    _____ to the _____ because it is the

    _____ of all consumers.

6. The less essential the product, the more _____

    is demand.

7. The monopolist must consider how many units of output can be sold

    at _____.

8. In a pure monopoly, the demand curve is also the _____

    curve for the firm.

9. For a product with inelastic demand, the monopolist can obtain a

    higher price and larger revenue by _____. If

    demand were elastic, it would be more profitable to _____

    _____.

10. The similarities between the cost curves of a monopolist and
    those of other producers are summarized below:

    • At first, the cost per unit decreases as the number of units

        produced _____.

    • When the increase in the AVC becomes great enough to offset the

        decrease in the AFC, the _____ increases.

124

● Production should be increased until the point where the MC

   of the next unit produced will be _____

   the corresponding MR.

11. Because the monopolist is faced with a(n) _____

    _____ AR curve, the MR curve will always be

    _____ the AR curve, and the MR curve will

    _____ at a faster rate.

12. The monopolist faces a situation where, in order to sell, _____

    _____

13. The AR of the monopolist declines because _____

    _____

    _____.

14. The MR declines at a faster rate than the AR because, in order to

    sell a larger number of units, the monopolist must accept _____

    _____ on the units that could have been sold at a

    higher price had the monopolist elected to sell fewer units.

15. Describe what would happen if a monopolist were unable to block

    the entry of additional firms into the industry. _____

    _____

    _____

16. When compared to pure competition, monopoly results in a higher

    _____, the use of fewer _____, and

    greater _____.

Restraints on Monopoly Price

17. The monopolist cannot charge more for a product than _____

_____.

18. Even if a firm is a monopoly, it cannot arbitrarily set a price

    and _____ at that price.

    ● The monopolist can _____ to attain the

      best possible price for itself.

    ● The price which is most profitable to the monopolist, and
      within the reach of few consumers, might keep a large number
      of consumers from enjoying the product.

19. List four major economic considerations that can deter the mono-
    polist from selling its goods at the highest possible price.

    (1) _____

    (2) _____

    (3) _____

    (4) _____

III. MONOPOLISTIC COMPETITION

1. Monopolistic competition is a market condition in which there are

   a relatively _____ number of firms supplying

   _____, with each firm having _____

   _____.

Differentiated Products

2. The major characteristic of monopolistic competition is product

   differentiation, which is the practice of _____

   _____

   _____

   _____.

3. Product differentiation gives an individual supplier a certain

   price range within which prices may be _____

   without substantially affecting either _____

   or _____. This is the _____

   aspect of monopolistic competition.

   • If, however, an individual supplier raises its prices too high

     above its competitors', it will lose consumers. If it sets its

     prices lower than the prices of its competitors, it will draw

     consumers away from the other brands. This is the _____

     _____ aspect of monopolistic competition.

4. In monopolist competition, there is usually an absence of strong
   price competition. Instead, firms employ the following
   strategies to sway consumers:

   (1) _____

   (2) _____

   (3) _____

5. Because of the large number of firms in a market characterized by

   monopolistic competition, there is little likelihood that firms

   will engage in collusive practices to _____ or to

   _____.

Short-run Price and Profit

6. The demand curve of an individual firm in a market characterized by monopolistic competition will slope _____ to the _____.

7. The demand curve for an individual firm will tend to be _____ _____ than the demand curve for the total industry.

   ● The more closely monopolistic competition approaches pure competition, the closer to _____ will be the demand curve of the individual firm.

   ● The more market conditions move in the direction toward _____ or _____, the _____ elastic the individual firm's demand curve will be and the more closely it will approach the industry demand curve.

8. When the demand or <u>AR</u> curve slopes downward to the right, the <u>MR</u> curve will move in the same direction, but _____.

Long-run Equilibrium

9. In monopolistic competition, if short-run profits are available in the industry,

   ● New firms will enter the market with their similar but _____ _____ products, causing the total supply on the market to _____.

   ● The market price will _____, lowering the _____ of each firm in the industry.

● So long as there are no _____ , the

process will continue until the profits for the average firm

will be _____ .

10. In monopolistic competition, if firms in the industry have been
suffering losses in the short run, then the following results
are likely:

_____

_____

_____

11. In the long run, under conditions of monopolistic competition,

consumers will receive a differentiated product at a price that

is equal to _____

_____ .

12. Even if costs were identical, the equilibrium price under

_____ would be higher than the

price under _____ .

● Graphically, this fact is explained by the _____

of the AR curve under monopolistic competition which prevents

the AR curve from touching the ATC curve at _____ .

IV.   OLIGOPOLY

1. Oligopoly is a market condition in which _____

_____ produce _____ .

2. There must be few enough firms that the actions of any one on

matters of _____ and _____ will have

a noticeable effect on the others.

3. The two basic characteristics of oligopoly are:

   (1) _____

   (2) _____

4. An increase in supply by any one firm would increase _____

   _____ and tend to _____.

5. If one firm cut its price, it would _____

   _____ at the expense of the other firms.

   ● The other firms might react by _____.

   ● This retaliation would affect all firms' _____,

   and might wipe out the initial gain of the price-cutting firm.

6. Whether or not firms would gain from price competition would

   depend on the _____.

7. Although an oligopolist may be reluctant to engage in price

   competition because of _____

   _____, many forms of nonprice

   competition (for example, _____

   _____) are found in oligopolies.

8. Oligopolistic conditions sometimes lead to collusive practices,

   such as _____, _____, and

   other techniques designed to _____ or to

   _____.

Price Determination

9. Pricing under oligopoly is difficult because the firm may or may not be able to determine _____

_____.

10. Oligopoly is often described as a market situation in which the number of sellers is so few that each must take into consideration _____.

11. When an oligopolist changes its prices, its competitors may choose to ignore the price change. If this is the case, the _____ and _____ curve for the individual firm will be known with a reasonable degree of accuracy.

12. A change in price by an oligopolist may be met by a similar change by rivals.

    ● The demand curve of the firm initiating the price change would be relatively inelastic.

    ● The gain in sales resulting from _____ will be lessened by the impact of competitors' reduced prices.

    ● A firm initiating a rise in price will not lose as many sales as it otherwise would, if rivals _____

    _____.

13. Define the term substitution effect. _____

_____

131

14. When an oligopolist changes price, rivals may respond by

imitating _____ but ignoring

_____ .

- In the face of this kind of response from rivals, the substitution effect would tend to be absent after a decrease in price but present after a price increase.

- The demand curve of the firm initiating the price change will

be a(n) _____ , representing the

fact that demand is _____ if price

moves downward and _____ when price moves

upward.

Price Rigidity

15. Because of the tendency toward price rigidity in oligopoly,

sellers seldom engage in _____ .

Instead, sellers place great emphasis on _____

and tremendous stress on _____ .

16. Sometimes oligopolists practice administered pricing. What is an

administered price? _____

_____

_____

17. The tendency toward price stability associated with oligopoly

often leads to _____ . This is especially

likely in conjunction with the following two conditions:

(1) _____

(2) _____

18. In oligopoly, the _____ demand, especially with

a(n) _____ curve, makes price competition unprofitable

not only for the _____ but also for the _____.

V.   PURELY COMPETITIVE VERSUS MONOPOLISTIC PRICING

1. State three reasons why a high degree of competition is
    beneficial for the consumer.

    (1) _____

    (2) _____

    (3) _____

2. A high degree of competition enables the consumer to purchase a

    good at a price equal to _____

    _____ for a given scale of

    operation.

3. As a result of the less than perfectly elastic demand, the long-

    run equilibrium price will be higher under any form of _____

    _____ than it will be under _____

    for identical cost conditions.

4. Assuming similar scales of operation for firms in each of the two

    markets, under pure competition, the price is _____

    and the supply is _____ than under monopolistic

    competition.

5. Oligopolies and monopolies generally operate at much larger scales of operations than do firms in monopolistic competition or pure competition.

   ● The larger scales of operation generally result in lower

   _____ curves.

   ● It is possible that an oligopoly or a monopoly could have an

   equilibrium price _____ than that possible under

   pure competitive conditions. Nevertheless, the monopolist's or

   oligopolist's price is not equal to the lowest point on

   _____ (as is the price of a

   firm under pure competition).

VI. COMPETITION AMONG CONSUMERS

1. Pure competition among consumers exists in cases in which the following four conditions prevail:

   (1) _____

   (2) _____

   (3) _____

   (4) _____

2. Define each of the following terms.

   ● Monopsony--_____

   ● Oligopsony--_____

   ● Monopsonistic competition--_____

   _____

Concentration Ratios

3. The concentration ratio is the percentage of _____

in a given industry that is accounted for by _____

_____.

4. Imperfect competition (which includes _____,

_____, and _____)

exists in a substantial portion of U.S. markets for goods and

services.

Workable Competition

5. The concept of workable competition implies that it is not

necessary to have all the conditions of _____

in order to serve the best interest of the consumer.

6. According to this concept, under the following conditions some
forms of imperfect competition may be workable:

(1) _____

(2) _____

(3) _____

Some economists add a fourth condition:

(4) _____

VII. ANTITRUST LAWS IN THE UNITED STATES AND CANADA

1. The purpose of antitrust laws is to maintain _____,

to prevent _____, and to restrict _____

_____.

Sherman Antitrust Act (U.S.)

2. The Sherman Antitrust Act of 1890 makes illegal "every

contract, combination,... or conspiracy" in _____.

3. Courts have generally held that restraint must be _____

   and _____ before it is illegal.

4. In interpreting this act, courts once held that mere bigness was

   not _____, but later decisions held that

   concentration of economic power was undesirable, even _____

   _____.

Clayton Act (U.S.)

5. The Clayton Act, passed in 1914, attempted to arrest the
   tendency toward corporate combinations by prohibiting the
   following four practices:

   (1) _____

   _____

   (2) _____

   _____

   (3) _____

   _____

   (4) _____

6. Although the Clayton Act states that "the labor of human beings

   is not _____ or _____,"

   the Supreme Court has held that the Sherman Act applied to

   _____ under certain conditions.

7. The Robinson-Patman Act of 1936 was primarily designed to

   prevent _____.

8. In 1950, the _____ Act (the _____ - _____

    Amendment) made it illegal for one corporation to acquire the

    assets, as well as the stock, of another company where the

    acquisition of such assets might

    (1) _____,

    (2) _____, or

    (3) _____.

Federal Trade Commission Act (U.S.)

9. The Federal Trade Commission Act of 1914 makes illegal any

    unfair _____ and gives the

    Federal Trade Commission the power to prevent the use of unfair

    methods in commerce.

10. The _____ - _____ Act of 1938 gave the Federal

    Trade Commission the power of initiative to restrain certain

    business practices, such as _____ and

    _____.

Combines Investigation Act (Canada)

11. Canadian anti-combines legislation seeks to eliminate _____

    _____ in order to stimulate maximum _____,

    _____, and _____ through _____.

12. The Combines Investigation Act of 1975 amends and consolidates
    most earlier legislation on this subject.

13. Three specific practices prohibited by this act are

(1) _____

(2) _____

(3) _____

14. The Combines Investigation Act makes it illegal to participate

in a merger or monopoly that is detrimental to _____,

_____, or _____.

TERMINOLOGY AND CONCEPTS INTRODUCED

pure monopoly--_____

_____

monopolistic competition--_____

_____

product differentiation--_____

_____

oligopoly--_____

_____

substitution effect--_____

_____

kinked demand curve--_____

_____

administered price--_____

_____

monopsony--_____

_____

oligopsony--_____

_____

monopsonistic competition--_____

_____

concentration ratio--_____

_____

workable competition--_____

_____

SAMPLE OBJECTIVE QUESTIONS

1. A pure monopoly is a theoretical set of market conditions. The
    following statements can correctly be made about a pure monopoly:

    A. The conditions of pure monopoly require that there be only a
        single seller in the market
    B. The conditions of pure monopoly require that there be no close
        substitutes for a good
    C. Government-regulated public utilities are a current example of
        pure monopolies
    D. In a pure monopoly, demand for the output of a single firm can
        be represented on a graph by a straight horizontal line

        (1) All of these
        (2) A, B and C only
        (3) A, B and D only
        (4) B, C and D only
        (5) A and D only

2. A producer operating under monopolistic market conditions can expect
    that, whenever the selling price of a product is decreased,

        (1) a larger number of units will be sold and marginal revenue will
            increase
        (2) a larger number of units will be sold and marginal revenue will
            decrease
        (3) a larger number of units will be sold and marginal revenue will
            remain constant
        (4) both the number of units sold and marginal revenue will remain
            constant

3. Pure competition and pure monopoly are the extremes in a wide range of market conditions, while monopolistic competition falls somewhere in the middle. Monopolistic competition is characterized by

   (1) absolute price control
   (2) product differentiation
   (3) a relatively small number of firms
   (4) a relatively small number of consumers

4. Oligopsony is a market condition in which

   (1) a few firms are the only suppliers of a unique product or service
   (2) only one buyer exists for a particular product or service
   (3) a single firm produces a small variety of products
   (4) a few consumers dominate the market for a particular good or service

5. One piece of United States legislation states that "the labor of human beings is not a commodity or article of commerce." At first this act was thought to exempt labor unions from antitrust action, but the Supreme Court held that antitrust legislation applied to unions under certain conditions. This act, which is often referred to as labor's Magna Carta, is the

   (1) Robinson-Patman Act
   (2) Sherman Antitrust Act
   (3) Federal Trade Commission Act
   (4) Clayton Act

ANALYSIS OF SAMPLE OBJECTIVE QUESTIONS

1. Choice (2) is the correct answer; statements A, B, and C are all correct. Statement D is a false statement, because the monopolist's demand curve slopes downward to the right. A straight horizontal line is the demand curve for an individual firm under conditions of pure competition.

2. The correct answer is choice (2). Choices (1), (3), and (4) are all incorrect. For the monopolist, the demand curve is also the average revenue (AR) curve. Because the demand curve of the monopolist is negatively sloped, as the price decreases, the number of units sold does not remain constant (4), but increases. Because the marginal revenue (MR) curve of the monopolist has a steeper slope than the AR curve, as the number of units sold increases, the MR will decrease, not increase (1) or remain constant (3).

3. Choice (2) is the correct answer. Although producers do have a limited degree of control over price in monopolistic competition, this control is by no means absolute, so choice (1) is wrong. Choice (3) is incorrect because there are a relatively large number of firms in monopolistic competition. The number of consumers (4) does not enter into the determination of whether or not an industry is characterized by monopolistic competition.

4. The correct answer is choice (4). Choices (1), (2), and (3) are all incorrect. Choices (1) and (2) are descriptions of oligopoly and monopsony, respectively. Choice (3) is incorrect because monopolistic competition involves a relatively large number of firms.

5. The correct answer is choice (4); choices (1), (2), and (3) are all incorrect. Choice (1) exhibits the characteristics of oligopoly, while choice (2) is a definition of monopsony. Choice (3) is incorrect because it focuses on the individual firm rather than on consumers.

REVIEW QUESTIONS

1. Why is it difficult for a pure monopoly to exist?

2. Compare the demand curve for an individual firm to that for the entire industry for each of the following markets: (a) pure monopoly, (b) monopolistic competition, (c) oligopoly.

3. Table 8-1 below compares the marginal revenue for a firm under conditions of pure competition to that for a monopolist. Compute the MR figures to complete the table. (A)

Table 8-1 Marginal Revenue--Pure Competition Versus Monopoly

Pure Competition				Monopoly			
Quantity	Price	TR	MR	Quantity	Price	TR	MR
1	$10	$10	--	1	$12	$12	--
2	10	20	$___	2	11	22	$___
3	10	30	$___	3	10	30	$___
4	10	40	$___	4	9	36	$___

4. Explain why the equilibrium price under monopolistic competition will always be higher than the equilibrium price under pure competition, even if costs are identical. (You may sketch graphs of cost curves to support your explanation.)

141

5. How does the number of firms in an industry promote or impede the development of collusive practices?

6. Use examples to illustrate each of the varying degrees of competition among consumers.

ANSWERS TO SELECTED REVIEW QUESTIONS

3.

Pure Competition		Monopoly	
Quantity	MR	Quantity	MR
2	$10	2	$10
3	10	3	8
4	10	4	6

(Under pure competition or monopoly, MR is computed by subtracting TR for the preceding quantity [Quantity -1] from TR for the quantity in question.)

9

Money and Economic Activity

OBJECTIVES

In this chapter, you will study the effect of money on the economy. You will become familiar with the monetary equation. You will learn of price indexes and how they can be used to determine the value of money. Upon completion of this chapter, you should be able to

- Identify the elements of the monetary equation

- Predict the impact of certain changes in the elements of the monetary equation

- Discuss the components and limitations of the Consumer Price Index (CPI)

- Explain the concept of real wages

- Describe the effects of price changes

WORKING OUTLINE

Introduction

1. Money not only facilitates _____ and _____, but the amount and flow of money also affect the circular flow of economic activity and the_____.

I.   **MONEY SUPPLY AND ECONOMIC ACTIVITY**

   The Monetary Equation

   1. The _____ attempts to explain the relation-ship between the quantity of money and the price level.

2. This theory assumes that any money received usually will be

    _____

    _____. Such a theory is an

    example of the _____.

3. This theory is expressed by the following formula:

    $$\underline{\hspace{2cm}} = \underline{\hspace{2cm}}$$

    ● <u>M</u> is the total money supply, including all _____

    _____.

    ● <u>V</u> is the velocity of money, or the _____

    _____

    _____. Velocity can be

    determined by dividing _____ into

    _____.

    ● <u>P</u> is the price level, or the _____

    _____. <u>P</u> has no practical value.

    ● <u>T</u> is the _____. For

    our purposes, <u>T</u> is the _____

    _____ produced and sold in the economy

    over a period of time.

4. The formula states that money times velocity, which equals the

    _____, is equal to the average

    price times the total units produced and sold.

5. Restate the monetary equation, isolating <u>P</u>.

    $$\underline{P} = \underline{\hspace{2cm}}$$

6. If the money supply remains stable and other things remain unchanged, there will be no change in either the _____
   _____ or the _____ .

7. The effect of change in the money supply will depend to some

   degree on the _____ .

8. In a full employment economy (that is, full employment of _____
   _____ , _____ , and
   _____), an increase in the total money supply
   will result in _____ .

9. At full employment, it is almost impossible to increase the total

   output of goods and services in the short run. Therefore, the

   additional money available will be used by individuals and firms

   to _____

   _____ .

   ● This situation causes prices to _____ , which will result

     in _____ .

10. An exception may result if individuals decide to _____
    the additional money they receive rather than to _____
    it. In this case, the _____ would decrease.

11. An increase in the money supply in an economy that is operating

    at less than full employment is likely to result in _____

    _____ instead of a

    rise in prices. As long as _____ were

increased in proportion to the increase in the money supply, the price level would remain stable.

12. An increase in the _____ of money can have an effect similar to that caused by an increase in the money supply. The two often occur simultaneously to compound the effect on the price level.

13. If individuals and firms were to increase their _____ when the money supply was increased, they could counteract the tendency of the increased money supply to _____ and/or _____.

14. A decrease in the money supply can bring about a reduction in the _____ and/or a decline in the _____.

15. The decrease in the price level could be offset by an increase in _____. Often, in a full-employment economy, individuals will increase _____ to compensate for a relative scarcity of _____.

16. Many times, however, a decrease in the money supply is accompanied by a decrease in _____, aggravating a(n) _____ decline.

17. If individuals spend income faster or save a smaller portion of it, the turnover of the total money supply will be greater and total spending will be _____. This could lead to an increase in the _____ _____ and/or a price increase, depending upon the circumstances existing in the economy.

18. A(n) _____ in velocity, which results from spending at a slower rate or saving a larger portion of income, will lead to a(n) _____ in production and/or a(n) _____ in prices.

19. Whenever investment is greater than _____, either an increase in economic activity or a rise in prices follow.

20. Unless there is a change in velocity, businesses can only increase their investment if there is an increase in the _____--either an increase in the amount of _____ or an increase in _____.

21. Government deficit spending is frequently financed by means of _____ which is generated by _____.

22. A decrease in bank credit which would reduce the money supply could be brought about by either _____ or _____.

II. CHANGES IN THE PRICE LEVEL

1. What purpose is served by a price index? _____

_____

_____

_____ Prices are determined for

_____, and the prices for all subsequent

years are measured in relation to _____.

A Hypothetical Price Index

2. In order for a price index to be accurate, both the _____

and the _____ of the items whose prices are to be

measured must remain constant.

3. A price index is a means of comparing prices at any time with the

level that existed in _____.

4. The index for any given year can be obtained by dividing the

_____ by the _____.

5. Any one year can be compared to another by _____

_____.

6. It is necessary to change the base year occasionally. Give three
   reasons why the comparison of current prices to prices in some
   earlier period would become meaningless if the base year went
   unchanged.

   (1) _____

   (2) _____

   (3) _____

7. A change in the base year does not change the _____,

but merely changes the year to which current prices are compared.

8. Occasionally, the products in the "market basket" analyzed by the index must change. List two reasons why the absolute cost of buying the new package of goods and services may be more or less than the absolute cost of buying the former package of goods and services.

    (1) _____

    (2) _____

The Consumer Price Index

9. The Consumer Price Index (CPI) compares the price of some of the basic commodities and services required by an average family of four in a moderate-sized community.

    ● Of the more than _____ items required, the

    Canadian CPI includes _____ and the CPI for the United States

    includes _____.

10. The items in the market basket are weighted according to _____

    _____

    to each of several categories.

11. A separate index is calculated for _____

    as well as _____.

12. List six categories included in the CPI market basket.

    (1) _____   (4) _____

    (2) _____   (5) _____

    (3) _____   (6) _____

149

13. Since prices of some goods and services rise faster than others, it is essential to use _____ and _____ when utilizing the index for specific purposes.

14. In the 1970s, the largest price increases in the United States were in _____, while in Canada the largest price increases were in the _____.

15. The CPI measures the _____ in the cost of living, not the actual cost of living. A higher index in one city may not necessarily indicate that prices are actually higher in that city than they are elsewhere.

16. The CPI is not a completely pure price index, which is to say that certain elements of _____ _____ are reflected in the index.
    - Various studies indicate that the size of the upward bias involved with the collection and processing of data for the index approximates _____ annually.

17. The CPI only endeavors to measure changes in the prices of _____, and these account for only about _____ of the total spending.

18. Give examples of the items the CPI does not take into account.

    _____

    _____

19. A price measure which is broader than the CPI is the _____ _____, which includes changes in the prices of all goods and services produced by a nation's economy.

20. There is an index which only measures changes in producer prices.
   - In Canada, this index is known as the _____ _____ (_____).
   - In the United States, the corresponding index is the _____ _____.

21. In recent years, much additional interest has been generated in the _____, _____, and _____ of the CPI.
   - Millions of industrial workers have their wages tied to the CPI through _____ clauses.
   - _____ and _____ are often adjusted for the cost-of-living changes.
   - The _____ programs in the United States are related to the CPI.

22. In Canada, federal income tax rates are adjusted annually for changes in the CPI, so that taxpayers are prevented from being pushed into _____ in the absence of growth in _____.

Value of Money

23. Price indexes are also useful in determining the value of money, which is based upon _____

    _____.

24. If prices rise, the value of money _____, and if prices fall, the value of money _____.

25. The value of a dollar in a given year can be determined by dividing the dollar by the _____ for that year and multiplying by _____.

26. In 1982, the value of the United States or Canadian dollar, using 1967 as the base year, was $_____.

Real Income

27. Although the purchasing power of the dollar has _____ in recent decades, people in the United States and Canada have _____ today than they had previously.

28. The total purchasing power of the average individual _____ in the 1950s and 1960s, but it _____ in the United States in the latter part of the 1970s and the early 1980s as _____ rose faster than incomes.

Effects of Price Changes

29. Persons whose incomes rise with increases in business activity

and prices benefit from _____, but are at a

disadvantage when prices are _____.

● Give two examples that fall into this category.

(1) _____ (2) _____

30. Persons whose incomes tend to remain fixed or relatively stable

in spite of changes in business conditions and prices suffer

during a period of _____, but they gain during a

period of _____, provided they maintain their _____

and their _____.

● List four types of persons in this category.

(1) _____ (3) _____

(2) _____ (4) _____

31. Changes in the price level also affect creditors and debtors,
each in a different manner.

● Inflation is beneficial to _____, but detrimental

to _____.

● Deflation is beneficial to _____, but detrimental

to _____.

TERMINOLOGY AND CONCEPTS INTRODUCED

quantity theory of money--_____

_____

transactions approach--_____

_____

money supply ($\underline{M}$)--_____

_____

velocity (<u>V</u>)--_____

_____

price level (<u>P</u>)--_____

_____

total transactions (<u>T</u>)--_____

_____

price index--_____

_____

Consumer Price Index (CPI)--_____

_____

GNP implicit price deflators--_____

_____

cost-of-living adjustment (COLA)--_____

_____

SAMPLE OBJECTIVE QUESTIONS

1. The following statements can correctly be made about the quantity theory of money:

   A. This theory assumes that any money received generally will be spent to buy goods and services
   B. This theory is expressed by the formula MV = PT
   C. This theory holds that total spending in the economy is equal to the price level or average price per transaction
   D. This theory holds that when there are sizable increases in the money supply in a period of full employment, the result might be inflation
   E. This theory suggests that an increase in the turnover of money in the economy can lead to an increase in the level of economic activity and/or price increases

      (1) All of these
      (2) A, B, D and E only
      (3) B, C, D and E only
      (4) A, B and E only
      (5) A, C and D only

2. Assume that the 1980 price index is 480, using 1967 as the base year. In 1980, the purchasing power of $1.00, expressed in 1967 dollars, is to the nearest cent

   (1) $.48
   (2) $.37
   (3) $.26
   (4) $.21

3. One difficulty involved in using the Consumer Price Index (CPI) to compare the cost of living in an area over a period of years is that the CPI

   (1) places too much emphasis on the changes in the prices of machinery, equipment, and raw materials
   (2) measures commodities only, and does not include basic services required by the consumer
   (3) does not weight the different components of the index in proportion to their average relative importance
   (4) is not a pure price index but also reflects some changes in the quality of commodities and services

ANALYSIS OF SAMPLE OBJECTIVE QUESTIONS

1. Choice (2) is the correct answer. Statements A, B, D, and E are all correct. Statement C is incorrect; the total spending in the economy is equal to the average price per transaction times the number of transactions.

2. Choice (4) is the correct answer. Choices (1), (2), and (3) are all incorrect. The formula for computing the index is

$$\text{Index} = \frac{\text{Cost in given year}}{\text{Cost in base year}}$$

Therefore, the cost of an item in the base year could be determined with the following formula:

$$\text{Cost in base year} = \frac{\text{Cost in given year}}{\text{Index}}$$

To find the purchasing power in base-year dollars (1967 dollars in this case) of $1.00 in the given year (1980 in this example), assume that the Cost in given year = $1.00. Then, this problem can be solved as follows:

$$\text{Cost in base year} = \frac{\$1.00}{\$4.80} = \$.208 \text{ or } \$.21$$

3. The correct answer is choice (4). Choice (1) is incorrect because the CPI does not measure price changes for machinery, equipment, and raw materials. The CPI does include the value of basic services and does weight the different components in proportion to their importance, so choices (2) and (3) are wrong answers.

REVIEW QUESTIONS

1. Assuming that $\underline{M}$ = \$10, $\underline{V}$ = 3, and $\underline{T}$ = 5, what is the value of $\underline{P}$? **(A)**

   a. If $\underline{M}$ is increased to \$20, and $\underline{V}$ and $\underline{T}$ remain unchanged, what happens to the value of $\underline{P}$? **(A)**

   b. If, during a period of less than full employment, $\underline{M}$ is increased to \$20, and $\underline{T}$ is increased to 10, and the value of $\underline{V}$ remains unchanged, what happens to the value of $\underline{P}$? **(A)**

   c. If $\underline{M}$ is decreased to \$8, and $\underline{V}$ and $\underline{T}$ remain unchanged, what happens to the value of $\underline{P}$? **(A)**

   d. If $\underline{M}$ is decreased to \$8, and $\underline{T}$ is decreased to 4, and the value of $\underline{V}$ remains unchanged, what happens to the value of $\underline{P}$? **(A)**

   e. If the values of $\underline{M}$ and $\underline{T}$ remain at \$10 and 5 respectively, but $\underline{V}$ increases to 4, what happens to the value of $\underline{P}$? **(A)**

   f. If the values of $\underline{M}$ and $\underline{T}$ remain at \$10 and 5 respectively, but $\underline{V}$ decreases to 2, what happens to the value of $\underline{P}$? **(A)**

2. List three conditions that tend to promote each of the following economic situations: (a) stable flow of economic activity and a stable price; (b) decrease in the level of economic activity and/or a decline in the price level; (c) increase in the level of economic activity and/or increase in the price level.

3. In 1977, the cost of a certain market basket of commodities was \$250. In 1981, the cost of those same commodities was \$385. Using 1977 as the base year, what is the 1981 index for these goods? **(A)**

4. Explain through example the effects of inflation and deflation on creditors and debtors.

ANSWERS TO SELECTED REVIEW QUESTIONS

1. $$P = \frac{\$10 \times 3}{5} = \frac{\$30}{5} = \$6$$

If the total spending in the economy is $30 ($10 turned over 3 times) and there are 5 transactions, then the price of the average transaction is $6.

(a) $$P = \frac{\$20 \times 3}{5} = \frac{\$60}{5} = \$12$$

When the money supply increases and there is no change in velocity or the number of transactions, the price level increases.

(b) $$P = \frac{\$20 \times 3}{10} = \frac{\$60}{10} = \$6$$

When the money supply increases and there is a corresponding change in the number of transactions, prices can remain level.

(c) $$P = \frac{\$8 \times 3}{5} = \frac{\$24}{5} = \$4.80$$

When the money supply decreases and there is no change in velocity or the number of transactions, the price level falls.

(d) $$P = \frac{\$8 \times 3}{4} = \frac{\$24}{4} = \$6$$

When the money supply decreases and there is a corresponding change in the number of transactions, prices can remain level.

(e) $$P = \frac{\$10 \times 4}{5} = \frac{\$40}{5} = \$8$$

If there is an increase in velocity while the money supply and the number of transactions are unchanged, the price level increases.

(f) $$P = \frac{\$10 \times 2}{5} = \frac{\$20}{5} = \$4$$

If there is a decrease in velocity while the money supply and the number of transactions are unchanged, the price level falls.

3. 1981 Index = ($385 ÷ $250) x 100 = 154

10
Money: Its Nature, Function, and Creation

OBJECTIVES

In this chapter, you will be introduced to the terminology used to describe money. You will study the uses of money and learn how the presence of demand deposits in banks leads to the multiple expansion of bank credit. Upon completion of this chapter, you should be able to

- Distinguish between full-bodied money and credit money

- Discuss the common measures of United States and Canadian money supply

- Identify the four functions of money

- Explain how an individual bank can increase the money supply

- Discuss the process known as multiple expansion of bank credit

- Describe the effects of changes in the reserve requirements imposed on banks

WORKING OUTLINE

Introduction

1. Many definitions of "money" exclude the largest portion of the money supply, which is _____.

2. Give a definition of "money" that is broad enough to include all segments of money supply. _____

_____

_____

I. THE NATURE OF MONEY

1. What is commodity money? _____

   _____

2. List and define the two types of modern commodity money.

   (1) _____

   (2) _____

Classification of Money

3. Full-bodied money is money in which the intrinsic value of the material content is _____ the monetary value (face value).

4. Credit money (_____) is money in which the intrinsic value of the material content is _____ the monetary value.

5. Most _____ in Canada and the United States is credit money.

6. Sometimes money that is not backed 100 percent by _____ is referred to as credit money.

7. Credit money can be issued by a government in the form of

   _____.

8. When government-issued credit money is backed by _____

   _____

   _____, it is referred to as fiat money.

159

9. At one time, Federal Reserve notes and Bank of Canada notes were partially backed by _____.
Today, this is no longer true.

10. Credit money also can be issued by banks in the form of _____ and _____.

11. The largest portion of the money supply of Canada and the United States is in the form of _____
(_____).

Measures of the Money Supply

12. Virtually all the money in the United States and Canada is _____.

13. Over 90 percent of the total currency of each nation is in the form of _____ and _____.
These notes are issued by the _____
and the _____.

● Such notes are obligations not only of the _____,
but also of the _____

● Although gold backing is no longer required for these notes,
many are still _____, with most of
the remainder secured by _____ or
certain other types of bank assets.

14. The remainder of the currency is composed of _____
_____.

15. In the United States, the common measures of the money supply are M1, M2, M3, and L. In the spaces below, write in the types of money that are included in each measure.

● M1 = _____

_____

_____

● M2 = _____

_____

_____

● M3 = _____

_____

_____

● L = _____

_____

_____

16. In Canada, the common measures of the money supply are M1, M1A, M2, and M3. In the spaces below, write in the types of money that are included in each measure.

● M1 = _____

_____

_____

● M1A = _____

_____

_____

● M2 = _____

_____

_____

● M3 = _____

_____

_____

II. FUNCTIONS OF MONEY

Standard of Value

1. Money serves as a standard of value or as a unit of _____

_____. This means that we can measure the value

of _____.

Medium of Exchange

2. Money serves as a medium of exchange and facilitates the

_____.

3. If it were not for money, the exchange of goods and services

would be on a barter basis and would be extremely cumbersome

because of the problem of _____.

Store of Value

4. How does money serve as a store of value? _____

_____

_____

5. List three reasons why it can be difficult to accumulate and hold
wealth in the form of commodities.

   (1) _____

   (2) _____

   (3) _____

6. In order for money to be a good store of wealth, it must possess

    _____.

Standard of Deferred Payment

7. For many purchases, consumers do not pay cash but agree to

    _____.

    Thus, money becomes a standard of deferred payment.

III. **CREATION OF CREDIT MONEY**

1. A primary deposit is created when individuals put money into
   their checking accounts.

   ● Such deposits are considered part of the money supply, but are

     offset by a decrease in _____

     _____.

2. A derivative deposit is created when individuals borrow money

   from a bank--that is, the deposit derives from _____.

   ● The bank creates a checking account for the person receiving
     the loan and then honors checks on the account, even though
     that account does not represent any extra cash.

Personal IOUs

3. Because personal IOUs are not _____, the

   issuer of such IOUs will find it difficult to operate on credit.

4. If merchants would accept IOUs as a medium of exchange, then the

   IOUs would be serving as a form of _____.

Demand Deposits

5. Why do banks usually give loans in some form other than legal tender currency? _____

_____

_____

6. Banks generally grant loans by creating _____

_____.

7. The borrower puts no money in the bank, but is able to write checks against the created _____.

8. These checks, which are _____ against the bank to pay _____, serve as money.

9. There is an increase in the money supply to the extent of

_____.

10. Since the bank does not lend cash, it might seem that there is no limit to the amount of loans which it can make in the form of _____. However, the bank will need to keep sufficient cash on hand to provide for _____

_____.

11. If _____, and if _____, the bank would need a reserve equal to the amount of checks written.

12. List three reasons why banks do not need such large reserves.

   (1) _____

   (2) _____

       _____

   (3) _____

       _____

13. The amount of checks that can be written and the extent of loans

   that can be made in the form of demand deposits are limited only

   by _____

   _____

   _____.

14. Banks are encouraged to make as many loans as is reasonably safe.

15. States, provinces, and bank regulators prevent abuses of the

   credit system by placing restrictions on the _____

   _____.

   • United States banks are generally required to keep _____

     _____ behind demand deposits.

   • As of September 1984, reserves for Canadian dollar demand

     deposits were set at _____, and

     reserves for Canadian dollar notice deposits were set at

     _____.

16. If a bank is required to keep a 10 percent cash reserve behind its demand deposits and if $100,000 is deposited in the bank, what two alternatives does the bank have?

(1) _____

_____

(2) _____

_____

 ● Which alternative is more profitable to the bank?

_____

 ● Which alternative would most banks follow?

_____

17. What difficulty does a bank encounter if it loans the maximum

amount it can loan? _____

_____

 ● What is an adverse clearing balance? _____

_____

 ● If a bank had reserves over and above the amount it is required to maintain, it might avoid an adverse clearing balance.

Multiple Expansion of Bank Credit

18. Even if the bank chooses the more conservative alternative,

there will be a(n) _____.

19. Although the individual bank could not loan the maximum amount

for fear of a(n)_____,

the banking system as a whole can loan the maximum amount, with-

out that fear.

Statements 20 through 25 relate to the situation given below.

Assume that a bank is required to keep a 12 percent cash reserve behind its demand deposits and that $100,000 is deposited in the bank.

20. Most likely, the bank will hold $_____ in cash as reserve and loan $_____ to its borrowers. **(A)**

21. This situation results in an increase in the money supply because of the presence of the $_____ that was originally deposited and the continued circulation of the $_____ in demand deposits as a result of the loan. **(A)**

22. If it were not fearful of an adverse clearing balance, the bank could hold $_____ in cash as reserve and loan approximately $_____ to its borrowers **(A)**

23. The bank system as a whole will hold $_____ in reserve and lend approximately $_____ in the form of demand deposits. **(A)**

24. Assume that all of the money that the first bank loaned finds its way into a second bank. That bank will most likely hold $_____ in cash as reserve and loan $_____ to its borrowers. **(A)**

25. This process will continue until various banks hold $_____

in cash as reserve and have loaned approximately $_____

in the form of demand deposits. **(A)**

* * * * * *

26. The process described in the preceding section is known as the

_____.

27. This process occurs whenever there is _____

_____.

28. Whenever there is a net withdrawal of deposits, a(n) _____

_____ occurs.

Effect of Changes in the Reserve Requirement

29. If banks were required to _____

_____, their ability to expand credit would

be reduced.

30. The relationship between _____

_____ and _____ is

known as the money multiplier. How is the money multiplier

calculated? _____

_____

31. _____ encourages

the acceleration or deceleration of the circular flow economic

activity.

SELECTED ANSWERS TO WORKING OUTLINE

II. CREATION OF CREDIT MONEY

Multiple Expansion of Bank Credit

20. $12,000; $88,000

21. $100,000; 88,000

22. $100,000; $733,300 ($100,000 ÷ .12 = $833,333; $833,333 x .88 = $733,333)

23. $100,000; $733,300

24. $10,560, $77,440 ($88,000 x .12 = $10,560; $88,000 x .88 = $77,440)

25. $100,000; $733,300

TERMINOLOGY AND CONCEPTS INTRODUCED

money--_____

_____

commodity money--_____

_____

metallic money--_____

_____

paper money--_____

_____

full-bodied money--_____

_____

credit money (token money)--_____

_____

fiat money--_____

_____

demand deposits (bank checking deposits)--_____

_____

double coincidence of wants--_____

_____

primary deposit--_____

_____

derivative deposit--_____

_____

adverse clearing balance--_____

_____

multiple expansion of bank credit--_____

_____

money multiplier--_____

_____

SAMPLE OBJECTIVE QUESTIONS

1. Assume that the only commercial bank in a community receives an
   original deposit of $100,000 and that it has a 10% reserve
   requirement. Theoretically, if this particular bank were to extend
   credit to the fullest extent possible, using this deposit as reserves,
   it could make loans in the form of demand deposits up to a maximum of

   (1) $ 10,000
   (2) $ 90,000
   (3) $100,000
   (4) $900,000

170

2. A bank is said to have an adverse clearing balance when the bank

   (1) holds less in cash reserves than the total amount of customer deposits
   (2) holds less in cash reserves than the total amount of outstanding customer loans
   (3) has had more money withdrawn than it has had deposited in a given period
   (4) has had more money withdrawn than it held in cash reserves in a given period

3. If an individual commercial bank is required to increase its reserve from 10 percent to 20 percent, the effect will be to

   (1) double the bank's ability to extend credit
   (2) reduce by approximately 50 percent the bank's ability to extend credit
   (3) increase by approximately 10 percent the bank's ability to extend credit
   (4) reduce by approximately 10 percent the bank's ability to extend credit

ANALYSIS OF SAMPLE OBJECTIVE QUESTIONS

1. The correct answer is choice (4). Choices (1), (2), and (3) are all incorrect. If the bank retains the entire $100,000 as reserves to back up demand deposits, it can lend an additional $900,000. In practice, however, an expansion of credit of this nature would more likely be accomplished through a network of banks.

2. Choice (3) is the correct answer. Choices (1), (2), and (4) are all incorrect. The determination of whether a bank has an adverse clearing balance does not depend upon the cash reserves, as stated incorrectly in (1), (2), and (4). For example, even if more money was withdrawn than the amount held in cash reserves, as in (4), the bank would not have an adverse clearing balance so long as cash deposits during this period more than outweighed the cash withdrawals.

3. Choice (2) is the correct answer. An increase in a bank's reserve requirement will not increase the bank's ability to extend credit, as in choices (1) and (3), but will reduce the amount it can lend. A doubling of the reserve requirement, from 10 percent to 20 percent, will cut in half the bank's ability to extend credit. In other words, it is not the absolute increase in the reserve requirement, as implied in choice (4), but the relative increase in the reserve requirement that will determine the extent of the reduction in the ability to extend credit.

REVIEW QUESTIONS

1. Using the terminology introduced in this chapter, describe a typical United States or Canadian dollar bill.

2. Use an example to illustrate the concept of double coincidence of wants.

3. Distinguish between a primary deposit and a derivative deposit.

4. If the reserve requirement is 12 percent, what is the money multiplier? **(A)**

ANSWERS TO SELECTED REVIEW QUESTION

4. 8.333 (1 ÷ .12 = 8.333)

11

Money Supply and
the Role of a Nation's Central Bank

OBJECTIVES

In this chapter, you will be introduced to the central bank of Canada and the central bank of the United States. You will study the measures a central bank can use to affect the money supply. Upon completion of this chapter, you should be able to

- State the function of each body within the Federal Reserve System

- Discuss the provisions of the United States Depository Institutions Deregulation and Monetary Control Act of 1980

- Describe the structure of the Bank of Canada

- Explain the impact of raising or lowering the reserve requirement

- Describe the process known as discounting

- Discuss the primary and secondary effects of raising or lowering the discount rate

- Explain the purpose of open-market operations

- Give examples of moral suasion

WORKING OUTLINE

Introduction

1. List four functions of a central bank.

   (1) _____

   (2) _____

   (3) _____

   (4) _____

2. Actions of the central bank affect not only other banks but also

   the _____ .

3. In the United States, the _____ ,

   popularly known as _____ , fulfills the

   role of a central bank. In Canada, the _____

   is the central bank.

I. STRUCTURE OF THE UNITED STATES FEDERAL RESERVE SYSTEM

1. The Fed is a(n) _____ of the government, yet it is

   not _____ by the government.

2. The Fed is owned by _____ , but its

   most important officials are appointed by _____ .

The Board of Governors of the Federal Reserve System

3. What is the primary function of the Board of Governors, or the

   Federal Reserve Board (FRB)? _____

   _____

4. The FRB consists of _____ members who are appointed by the

   _____ with the consent of

   _____ .

5. Each member must be selected from _____

   _____ .

6. Each member is appointed for _____ years and is

   eligible for _____ .

7. The _____ selects the chairman

   and the vice-chairman of the Board.

8. One power of the FRB is the supervision of the Federal Reserve
   Banks. List five of the FRB's duties in this capacity.

   (1) _____

   (2) _____

   (3) _____

   (4) _____

   (5) _____

Federal Reserve Banks

9. The Fed divides the United States into _____

   _____.

   ● The districts are organized on the basis of _____

   _____.

10. Each Federal Reserve Bank is controlled by _____

    _____.

    ● A majority of the members of the _____

    of each Federal Reserve Bank are nonbankers.

11. The board of directors for each Reserve Bank appoints a president
    and a vice-president for the Bank.

    ● These officers must be approved by _____

    and are responsible for _____

    _____.

175

12. List two duties of Federal Reserve Banks with regard to member banks.

    (1) _____

    (2) _____

13. In the event that any member bank chronically engages in unsound banking practices, the Reserve Bank has the authority to _____

_____.

14. Federal Reserve Banks serve as _____ for the federal government. List two duties of the Reserve Banks in this capacity.

    (1) _____

    (2) _____

15. List two other duties of Federal Reserve Banks.

    (1) _____

    (2) _____

Federal Reserve Member Banks

16. Commercial banks that belong to the System are called _____

_____.

17. Each national bank must be a member of the System or _____

_____.

18. Membership is open to state banks that can qualify. List three reasons why state banks might not join the system.

    (1) _____

    (2) _____

    (3) _____

19. Although less than _____ of all commercial banks

    belong to the System, these member banks do 70 to 75 percent of

    the total commercial banking business in the United States.

Obligations and Benefits of Membership

20. List six obligations of member banks.

    (1) _____

    (2) _____

    (3) _____

    (4) _____

    (5) _____

    (6) _____

21. In addition, member banks are subject to _____

    and _____ by the Federal Reserve Banks.

22. List five benefits of membership in the Federal Reserve System.

    (1) _____

    (2) _____

    (3) _____

    (4) _____

    (5) _____

U.S. Monetary Control Act of 1980

23. The United States Congress enacted the Depository Institutions Deregulation and Monetary Control Act of 1980 to _____

    _____ .

    ● List four types of depository institutions

    (1) _____ (3) _____

    (2) _____ (4) _____

24. The act permits all financial institutions to have _____

    _____ and _____ .

25. S & Ls are allowed to extend their loan business beyond

    _____ .

26. The act permits the payment of _____ .

27. It provided for the phase-out of all limitations on _____ .

28. _____ and _____ insurance coverage was increased to

    $100,000 per account.

29. The act requires that all depository institutions be subject to

    the _____

    _____ .

30. S & Ls are permitted to _____

    if necessary.

31. The Federal Reserve Banks will act as _____ for

    all depository institutions.

32. The act requires Federal Reserve Banks to charge fees to

_____ for certain Fed

services.

33. What are the two major purposes of the Monetary Control Act?

(1) _____

(2) _____

Federal Reserve Policy

34. Because the Fed is an independent organization, it may not always

agree with the economic policies of _____

_____, yet there is no formal

procedure for resolving any serious disagreements that arise.

35. However, since the objectives of the Fed and of the Administra-

tion are _____ and _____

_____, their actions usually complement

each other.

II. THE BANK OF CANADA

1. The Bank of Canada is _____ by the

Canadian government and serves as Canada's _____.

2. The Bank of Canada was established to be a bankers' bank. List
   two of the primary functions of the Bank.

(1) _____

(2) _____

3. The Bank is steered by a board of directors composed of _____

_____ .

 ● The directors are federally appointed for _____ -year terms

   by Canada's _____ .

 ● The _____ appoint the Governor and Deputy Governor

   for _____ -year terms.

 ● The Deputy Minister of Finance is a non-voting member of the

   board and serves mainly as _____

   _____ .

4. The actual governing body of the board of directors is the

   executive committee, composed of _____

   _____ .

 ● The committee's decisions must be submitted to the board for
   ratification.

5. The _____ has veto power over any

   decision of the executive committee or the board of directors.

 ● Any such veto must be reported to _____

   and is subject to approval by the _____ .

6. The Bank's economic policies are set jointly by _____

   and _____ ; in case of conflict, the _____

   _____ has ultimate authority.

Chartered Banks

7. All commercial banks operating in Canada are chartered by the

   _____ under the terms of the Bank Act.

8. Until 1981, when Canada liberalized its laws relating to bank chartering, there were only _____ chartered banks in Canada.

9. The Bank of Canada leaves the allocation of bank and other forms of credit to the _____.

    ● Each chartered bank is free to _____,

      thereby attempting to gain as large a share as possible of the

      _____.

10. Chartered banks are free to decide the proportion of their funds that they will _____

    and that they will _____.

Bank of Canada Monetary Policy

11. In using the powers at its disposal, the Bank of Canada attempts

    to _____

    _____

    _____.

12. What basic principle does the Bank rely upon in fostering favor-able economic conditions? _____

    _____

    _____

    _____

13. To move toward that goal, the Bank formerly set a range for

    _____ as measured by M1.

    ● M1 became a(n) _____ indicator of the financial

      environment.

- Major shifts of funds into and out of M1 balances were induced by financial innovations, such as _____ _____ and _____.

- Currently, the Bank of Canada no longer has a specific target for the _____.

14. The Bank of Canada can utilize its powers to affect bank credit by _____ _____.

15. The Bank can alter the level of cash reserves of chartered banks by one of the following methods:

    (1) _____ _____

    (2) _____ _____

16. The Bank may make loans or advances for periods not exceeding _____ to chartered banks or to certain savings banks on the pledge of _____.

17. Although the Bank of Canada operates with a large measure of independence, the Canadian government is still ultimately responsible for the general thrust of _____ _____.

18. The Bank of Canada Act of 1967 clarified the _____

    of the Bank and the government.

    ● The act provides for regular consultation between _____

       _____ and _____.

    ● In the event of a disagreement that cannot be resolved, the

       government may _____.

Federal Business Development Bank

19. The Federal Business Development Bank assists in the development

    of _____ in Canada by

    providing financial and management services.

20. List two qualifications that businesses should have to qualify
    for this financing.

    (1) _____

    (2) _____

21. In the United States, similar functions are performed by

    _____.

III. CENTRAL BANK CONTROL OF THE MONEY SUPPLY

1. The central bank can affect the money supply through its control

   over _____ and _____.

2. There are two types of measures through which the central bank
   controls bank credit.

   (1) _____ controls affect the overall supply of money.

   (2) _____ controls affect the use of money for specific

       purposes in the economy.

IV.   GENERAL CONTROLS

1. General controls can influence the total _____ and

    _____ of credit and money.

2. Occasionally, the use of general controls may cause an adverse
    effect on some specific activity. If offsetting measures are not
    available, the benefits derived from the general controls must be
    weighed against the ill effect(s) on the specific activity.

Reserve Requirements

3. The amount of reserve that must be held by commercial banks, as

    determined by the central bank, is known as the _____.

4. Any reserve over and above this amount that a bank may have is

    a(n) _____.

5. For purposes of setting reserve requirements, deposits in the
    United States are divided into two broad categories.

    (1) Transaction accounts are those _____

        _____. List five examples of trans-

        action accounts:

        (1) _____

        (2) _____

        (3) _____

        (4) _____

        (5) _____

    (2) Nonpersonal time deposits include _____

        _____

        _____.

6. In the United States, reserves against transaction accounts are
    to be _____ percent on the first $_____ and ____ to _____
    percent on deposits in excess of $_____ million. The $_____
    million breaking point will be adjusted annually by formula.

7. The FRB can impose a "supplemental" reserve of up to _____
    percent under certain conditions. The Fed pays interest on
    supplemental reserves.

8. Reserve requirements against nonpersonal time deposits are set by
    the FRB at between _____ and _____ percent.

9. In Canada, the Bank Act requires that each bank maintain a
    stipulated minimum amount of cash reserves as a percentage of its
    _____.

    ● These reserves must be in the form of _____
      _____ and _____
      _____.

    ● Recently, the reserve requirement was 10 percent on _____
      _____ and 1 percent on _____.

10. The Bank of Canada may require the chartered banks to maintain
    a secondary reserve, composed of _____, _____,
    and _____.

    ● The secondary reserve cannot exceed _____ percent.

11. During periods when production, income, and employment are low,

    the central bank in either country may _____

    _____ in the hope of increasing the

    _____ and bringing about an expansion of

    business activity.

    ● If the banking system has no excess reserves, so that it cannot
      create any more credit, and the central bank lowers the reserve
      requirement, part of the existing required reserve would become
      excess reserve. Then the banking system could extend
      additional money in demand deposits.

12. The reduction of the reserve requirement does not necessarily

    increase credit or the money supply, but merely _____

    _____ .

    There will not be an increase in credit or in the money supply

    unless and until _____

    _____

    ● Frequently in a period of slackness or recession, business-

      people are reluctant to borrow and spend money because of

      _____

      _____ .

13. The central bank can decrease the banks' ability to expand the

    money supply by _____ .

    ● If the banking system has no excess reserves and the central

      bank increases the reserve requirement, banks would actually

      be _____ .

● The banks might increase their reserves by recalling _____

_____, thus decreasing the _____

_____.

14. The central bank would not be likely to raise the reserve

requirement because such an action would _____

_____.

15. The central bank attempts to use its power to prevent undesirable
conditions from developing.

● It may try to ease the money supply by lowering _____

_____ when the economy enters a

period of _____ business activity.

● When the economy begins to reach the full employment,

or the _____, stage of business

activity, the central bank may endeavor to _____ the

money supply by _____ reserve require-

ments. At this stage, further increases in the money supply

through the extension of demand deposits probably will lead to

_____.

16. The central bank is rather cautious in the use of reserve re-

quirements to control credit. The reserve requirement is usually

changed by only _____

at a time. What is the primary reason for this caution?

_____

_____

_____

Discount Rate (Bank Rate)

17. The discount rate is the term used in the United States for the

    _____

    _____. The

    corresponding rate in Canada is _____.

18. Define the term <u>commercial paper</u>. _____

    _____

19. Describe the two methods by which a bank may borrow from the
    central bank. Include in each description the term used to refer
    to money borrowed in this manner.

    (1) _____

    _____

    _____

    (2) _____

    _____

    _____

    ● Which method is more popular? _____

    More convenient? _____

    ● Today both methods are generally referred to as _____

    _____.

20. In both methods, the discount rate governs the _____

    _____.

21. Discount facilities are a(n) _____ of the
    bank rather than a right.

22. Credit through this process is extended primarily on a short-
    term basis to enable a bank to adjust its reserve position
    when necessary because of such developments as _____
    _____ or _____.

23. If the interest rate charged by the central bank were equal to
    the rate the individual bank charges on the notes, the bank would
    _____ on its own loans to individuals and
    businesses.

24. When the discount rate is _____ compared to the commercial
    loan rate, the banks will be reluctant to use this discounting
    process to build up or replace their reserves. When the discount
    rate is _____, banks will be more inclined to replace or
    build up their reserves by discounting.

25. Since reserves increase the banks' ability to extend credit, a(n)
    _____ in the discount rate may bring about
    an increase in the money supply.

26. If an individual bank has no excess reserves, it can build up its
    reserves through the _____ process,
    and then it will be able to make further loans.

27. If the discount rate is lower than the interest rate on

commercial paper, then it is profitable for an individual bank

to discount _____, to build up

_____, and to make _____.

- The bank will net a small amount of interest on the original
notes, plus it will be able to earn interest on the new loans
it can make.

28. The lower the discount rate, the more it will profit individual
banks to discount, thus expanding the money supply. If the discount rate is equal to or greater than the commercial rate, it
will not be profitable for individual banks to discount.

29. The central bank can encourage banks to _____

or _____ credit by changes in the discount rate.

- Changes in the discount rate do not automatically lead to

changes in the money supply; businesses and individuals

must _____ to make changes in

the money supply effective.

30. A secondary effect of changing the discount rate is that such

changes influence the _____.

31. Define the prime loan rate. _____

_____

How does this rate usually compare to the discount rate? _____

_____

32. When business activity is falling, the central bank _____

    the discount rate to encourage banks to discount and increase

    their ability to expand credit, and the banks encourage

    businesses to borrow by _____ the commercial

    loan rate.

33. During full-employment inflationary periods, the central bank may

    _____ the discount rate to discourage discounting, which

    in turn has a restrictive effect on the expansion of credit and

    discourages borrowing by _____ commercial

    loan rates.

34. The discount rate is usually changed by very moderate amounts,

    such as _____,

    at a time, so that the change will not cause a serious disruption

    in business activity.

35. The central bank changes the discount rate as a(n) _____

    _____ measure rather than as a remedial measure.

    ● Sometimes changes in the discount rate lag behind changes in

      the _____.

    ● At such times, the central bank may raise or lower the

      discount rate to _____.

36. In Canada, the bank rate is set and published by the _____

    _____ for the entire country.

37. In the United States, the discount rate for each district is
    determined by its _____
    with the approval of the _____.

    ● The discount rate often varies slightly between districts for
      short periods because of _____

      _____.

    ● Usually when a district changes its rate, most of the others
      follow suit, since _____

      generally cause the change.

38. The direction and amounts of changes in the Fed discount rate and
    the Canadian bank rate are usually similar, since _____

    _____

    _____.

Federal Funds Market

39. In addition to borrowing from the central bank, a bank can adjust
    its reserve position by _____

    _____.

40. In the United States, interbank borrowing takes place in a
    fairly well-organized market, known as the _____

    _____.

41. What is federal funds rate? _____

    _____

    _____

42. The central bank has some control over the federal funds rate.

43. The federal funds rate is a very sensitive indicator of the
_____. It may be higher or
lower than the prevailing rate at the discount window, depending
on _____.

Open-Market Operations

44. One of the most important and continuously used instruments of
_____ is open-market operations.

45. The central bank has control over a portfolio consisting of
_____.

46. All commercial banks hold government obligations, and the central
bank can induce commercial banks to sell or buy government
securities by _____
_____.

47. If the central bank wants to encourage the expansion of credit,
it can buy securities held by commercial banks. This action
_____ the excess reserves of the
commercial banks and permits them to expand credit.

48. The central bank can achieve practically the same result by
purchasing securities from individuals or businesses, since
these sellers will usually _____
_____.
These deposits increase bank reserves and enable banks to expand
credit.

193

49. The potential expansion of credit is somewhat less when the central bank buys securities from individuals or businesses than when the central bank buys securities from commercial banks.

   ● When securities are purchased from commercial banks, the entire purchase amount can be used as excess reserves against potential demand deposits.

   ● When securities are purchased from individuals or businesses and these sellers deposit the purchase amount in commercial banks, the banks must hold a portion of this amount in required reserves; therefore, an amount less than the purchase amount can be used as excess reserves against potential demand deposits.

50. During times of _____, the central bank may wish to

   absorb some of the excess reserves held by commercial banks by

   _____ to the banks.

   ● To buy bonds, banks will most likely have to give up some

   _____, which in turn will _____

   their ability to extend credit.

51. If the central bank sells bonds to individuals or businesses, it

   assumes that they will _____ to pay for

   the bonds.

   ● Such withdrawals will reduce _____

   and _____ the banks' ability to extend credit.

52. The central bank's ability to affect the money supply through its open-market operations is restricted. State one restriction that applies to the central bank's purchasing securities and one that applies to its selling securities.

   (1) _____

   _____

   (2) _____

   _____

194

Moral Suasion

53. <u>Moral suasion</u> is the term applied to a host of different measures that the central bank uses to _____

_____.

54. Give four examples of moral suasion.

(1) _____

_____

(2) _____

_____

(3) _____

_____

(4) _____

_____

55. In general, moral suasion will affect the money supply only to the extent that _____

_____.

V. SELECTIVE CONTROLS

1. In the United States, the Fed does have certain discretionary controls that affect the specific uses of money and credit in the economy.

2. The Fed currently has the authority to set stock margin require-

ments, that is, the maximum amount of stock that may be _____

_____.

- The higher the margin requirement, the _____ the down

payment required to purchase shares of stock.

• High margin requirements reduce the opportunity for _____

_____, hold down the _____

_____, and moderate the _____.

3. In the past, the Fed has had control of the conditions or terms of installment sales. Such controls, which established the _____ and the _____ _____, had the effect of limiting total demand.

4. Canada has similar controls on installment loans.

TERMINOLOGY AND CONCEPTS INTRODUCED

member banks-- _____

_____

general controls-- _____

_____

selective controls-- _____

_____

required reserve-- _____

_____

excess reserve-- _____

_____

transaction accounts--_____

_____

nonpersonal time accounts--_____

_____

discount rate--_____

_____

bank rate--_____

_____

commercial paper--_____

_____

discounts--_____

_____

advances--_____

_____

prime loan rate--_____

_____

Federal Funds Market--_____

_____

open-market operations--_____

_____

moral suasion--_____

_____

SAMPLE OBJECTIVE QUESTIONS

1. The Board of Governors of the Federal Reserve System has as its primary function the formulation of a monetary policy for the United States economy. The following can correctly be listed as authorized powers of the Board:

   A. The Board establishes the international exchange rate for Unite States currency
   B. The Board approves or disapproves the appointment of officers (the Federal Reserve Banks
   C. The Board establishes reserve requirements within legal limits for all member banks
   D. The Board authorizes loans between Federal Reserve Banks

   (1) All of these
   (2) A, B and C only
   (3) A, B and D only
   (4) B, C and D only
   (5) C and D only

2. Within the decision-making structure of the Bank of Canada, the Governor of the Bank of Canada has the power to veto decisions that are made. However, the Governor's veto can be overturned by the

   (1) board of directors of the Bank
   (2) executive committee of the board of directors of the Bank
   (3) federal cabinet
   (4) Deputy Minister of Finance

3. The following statements can correctly be made about the Bank of Canada and Canadian chartered banks:

   A. Less than one-half of all Canadian banks are chartered under the terms of the Bank Act, but these banks are responsible for a majority of the commercial banking business
   B. Chartered banks are free to decide the proportion of their funds that they will invest in particular kinds of securities
   C. Each chartered bank is required to maintain a stipulated minimum amount of cash reserves as a percentage of its Canadian dollar deposit liabilities
   D. Although the Bank of Canada establishes a separate bank rate for each province in Canada, the variations between the rates are slight

   (1) A, B and D only
   (2) A, C and D only
   (3) B, C and D only
   (4) A and C only
   (5) B and C only

4. The Federal Reserve System, like other central banks, uses general controls and selective controls for regulating the supply of money in the economy. An example of a general control used by the Federal Reserve is

   (1) controlling the terms of installment sales
   (2) adjusting the federal funds rate
   (3) setting the prime rate for corporate loans
   (4) setting the stock market margin requirements

5. A central bank has at its disposal several courses of action which can effect the level of economic activity. Although such actions do not have a guaranteed effect, a central bank is likely to try to combat inflation by

   A. Buying government bonds on the open market
   B. Lowering the reserve ratio required of commercial banks
   C. Raising the discount rate (bank rate)
   D. Requesting commercial banks to restrict their lending

      (1) A, B and D only
      (2) A, C and D only
      (3) B, C and D only
      (4) A and B only
      (5) C and D only

ANALYSIS OF SAMPLE OBJECTIVE QUESTIONS

1. The correct answer is choice (4). Statements B, C, and D are all correct. Statement A is incorrect because the Federal Reserve Board is not responsible for establishing the exchange rate for United States currency.

2. Choice (3) is the correct answer. Choices (1), (2), and (4) are all incorrect. If the Governor of the Bank of Canada vetoes a decision of the executive committee or the board of directors, such a veto is subject to approval by the federal cabinet.

3. Choice (5) is the correct answer; statements B and C are both correct. Statement A is incorrect because all commercial banks operating in Canada are chartered by the Canadian federal parliament under the terms of the Bank Act. The Bank of Canada establishes a single bank rate for the entire country; therefore, statement D is false.

4. The correct answer is choice (2). Controlling the terms of installment sales (1) and setting the stock market margin requirements (4) are two examples of selective controls used by the Federal Reserve. The prime rate (3) is set by individual commercial banks; therefore, the prime rate is not directly under the control of the Federal Reserve.

5. Choice (5) is the correct answer; statements C and D are both correct. Statements A and B are actions that a central bank would take to stimulate a depressed economy; taking such actions during a period of inflation would likely aggravate the inflationary pressures.

REVIEW QUESTIONS

1. Referring to Figures 11-2, 11-3, 11-4, 11-5, and 11-6 in the textbook, explain in your own words the effects of changes in the reserve requirement.

2. Assume that the central bank increases the reserve requirement causing a decrease in commercial banks' ability to extend credit. Is it possible that an increase in the money supply could still occur? Explain your answer.

3. Referring to Figures 11-7 and 11-8, explain in your own words the benefits a commercial bank derives from a process known as discounting.

4. Referring to Figures 11-9, 11-10, and 11-11, explain in your own words the impact of a central bank's purchase of securities from banks and from individuals or businesses.

12

GNP and National Income

OBJECTIVES

In this chapter, you will study the various measures used to assess a nation's economy. You will be introduced to methods for determining the gross national product and you will see how the gross national product can be used to measure the standard of living. Upon completion of this chapter, you should be able to

- Distinguish among the gross national product, the net national product, national income, personal income, and disposable personal income

- Relate the allocation of and the sources of the gross national product to the circular flow of economic activity

- State why the gross national product is computed on a quarterly basis

- Identify the adjustments that must be made in the gross national product if it is to be an accurate measure of economic progress or of standard of living

- Explain the difference between a country's gross national product and its flow of funds

WORKING OUTLINE

I. **THE GROSS NATIONAL PRODUCT**

1. The dollar value of total production in an economy can be

   determined by adding the value of _____

   _____

   produced during a given period.

2. It is sometimes difficult to distinguish <u>intermediate products</u> from <u>end products</u>. Define each of these terms.

    ● Intermediate products--_____

    _____

    ● End products--_____

    _____

3. In counting the value of all the end products, it is possible

    that some items may be _____. For

    accuracy in calculating the total production, however, it is

    essential that _____.

4. According to the value-added method, the total production of an

    economy is equal to the summation of the total value added to all

    the products by the various producers plus the _____

    _____.

    ● The value added to a product by a producer is the difference

      between the _____ and the _____

      _____.

    ● This difference represents the amount that must be paid for

      _____, _____, and _____, as

      well as the _____ the producer will receive on

      the product.

5. The value-added method, though not actually used to measure
    production, can highlight the inaccuracies caused by double
    counting.

    ● If the value of a manufactured product were computed by adding
      the value at the end of each stage of production, there would

be much double counting. Therefore, the value obtained in that manner would be much greater than the true value of production as determined by the value-added method.

6. List the two principal points of view from which production is measured.

   (1) _____

   _____

   (2) _____

   _____

7. The gross national product (GNP) is defined as the current

   market value of _____

   _____.

   • Current market value, in this definition, means the _____

   _____

   _____.

8. The GNP is stated on a(n) _____ basis.

9. Total production each year uses up a certain amount of capital

   goods as _____, _____, _____,

   and _____ depreciate or become obsolete and lose

   their value.

   • The term for the amount of depreciation and obsolescence in

     capital goods is _____

     _____.

   • This amount is generally about _____ percent of total pro-

     duction.

10. The GNP minus the capital consumption allowance equals the

_____(NNP).

National Income

11. The national income (NI) is the total factor costs of _____

_____.

- According to this definition, NI is equivalent to the amount

that was paid for the use of _____, _____, _____,

and _____ to obtain a given GNP.

12. NI can also be defined as the aggregate _____

_____.

- From this perspective, NI is equivalent to the _____

_____ which were

used in producing the GNP.

13. The value of NI can be obtained in either of the following ways:

(1) _____

_____

(2) _____

_____

Personal Income

14. Personal income (PI) is the _____

_____.

15. PI includes transfer payments from _____

_____, but it excludes transfer payments among

_____.

● Define <u>transfer payment</u>. _____

_____

16. Not only individuals, but also _____

   are classified as "persons" for the purpose of determining PI.

17. PI is measured on a(n) _____ basis.

18. The following seven items are among those included in PI:

   (1) _____   (5) _____

   (2) _____   (6) _____

   (3) _____   (7) _____

   (4) _____

19. Identify the three segments of corporate profit and, for each
   segment, state whether it is considered part of PI or is subtracted from NI in determining PI.

   (1) _____

   (2) _____

   (3) _____

20. The computation of PI also involves the following three elements.
   For each element, tell whether it is included in (added to NI) or
   excluded from (subtracted from NI) in determining PI.

   (1) Personal interest income--_____

   (2) Public pension payments--_____

   (3) Net interest--_____

Disposable Personal Income

21. Disposable personal income (DPI) is what remains of personal income after deductions for _____

_____.

22. DPI is sometimes referred to as _____,
but this term is more frequently applied to that portion of disposable income remaining to a person after paying such items as

_____

_____.

Allocation of the Gross National Product

23. The GNP is allocated to four major sectors of the economy:

    (1) _____   (3) _____
    (2) _____   (4) _____

24. Private investment is that part of total production in the form

    of _____

    _____.

25. Net exports represent the difference between _____
    _____ and _____.

26. For each of the following sectors of the economy, state the approximate percentage of the 1982 United States output that was in that form.

    (1) Consumer goods and services--_____

    (2) Private investment--_____

    (3) Net exports--_____

    (4) Government expenditures--_____

206

27. For each of the following sectors of the economy, state the approximate percentage of the 1982 Canadian output that was in that form.

(1) Consumer goods and services--_____

(2) Private investment--_____

(3) Net exports--_____

(4) Government expenditures--_____

Sources of the Gross National Product

28. When the four sectors of the economy purchase goods and services, they must pay for them; these payments are then used to _____

_____

_____.

29. In the United States and Canada, payments to which factor of production account for approximately three-fourths of the distribution of NI? _____

Quarterly Reports on the GNP

30. The _____ and _____

_____ publish quarterly reports on the GNP and related figures. Give two reasons for this practice.

(1) _____

(2) _____

31. The quarterly reports are expressed in annual rates. How are these annual rates determined? _____

_____

32. The quarterly system makes it easier to analyze movements in the GNP.

   • _____ and _____ in the economy can be

     recognized at an earlier date than they would be if the GNP

     were published on a yearly basis only.

33. The GNP is frequently revised. Identify the three stages involved in calculating a final GNP figure.

   (1) _____

   (2) _____

   (3) _____

34. The data used to compute the GNP and related figures are _____

   _____ rather than _____.

GNP and the Circular Flow

35. The GNP is produced by _____,

   who in turn make payments to the _____

   for the contributions each factor makes to the GNP.

36. Incomes received by the factors of production are used to

   _____.

II. GNP AS A MEASURE OF ECONOMIC PROGRESS

   1. If the GNP is to be an accurate measure of either _____

     or _____, certain adjustments must be made

     in the GNP to reflect various changes which occur in the economy.

Changes in the Price Level

2. GNP can be increased merely by _____

    _____.

3. To obtain valid information when comparing one year with another,

    it is necessary to remove _____

    from _____.

4. The index known as GNP implicit price deflators considers not

    only _____ but also _____

    _____.

5. The GNP implicit price deflators allow economists to adjust the
    prices of all commodities in the economy simultaneously.

6. The current GNP can be adjusted to a real GNP, or a GNP in

    _____, by dividing the _____

    by the value of the _____.

7. Implicit price deflators allow economists to determine what
    portion of an increase in the current dollar GNP is due to infla-
    tion and what portion is due to true growth.

Changes in the Population Size

8. When there is an increase in the physical amount of goods and

    services during a period when the population is increasing, these

    goods and services are _____

    _____.

9. To adjust the real GNP for the increase in population, an economist could divide the _____ by the _____.

10. To obtain a better measure of the average amount of goods and services received per person, an economist could reduce GNP to _____, and then divide by _____. This computation results in the _____.

11. If the per capita DPI is adjusted for _____, the result is the real per capita DPI.

12. A comparison of the real per capita DPI for any two years will indicate any changes in the _____.

13. Although the real per capita DPI is not a perfect measure, it is the best measure of the _____ or of the _____.

Value of Nonmonetary Transactions

14. For the most part, the GNP takes into account only goods and services for which _____.

15. Goods and services that do not involve monetary transactions are just as important to the _____ as most of the items that are counted in the GNP.

16. It is estimated that activities equivalent to 10 to 15 percent of

the reported GNP are currently taking place in the United States

underground (subterranean) economy. What is an underground

economy? _____

_____

Types of Goods and Services Produced

17. The nature of some goods and services is such that individuals
cannot raise their standard of living by consuming these goods
and services. List four examples of such goods.

   (1) _____ (3) _____

   (2) _____ (4) _____

18. In comparing the GNP of various years to get an indication of the

change in the standard of living, an economist must consider the

_____

in each of those years.

19. An economist attempting to compare the standard of living in two

different countries by studying the respective values of their

GNPs must consider the types of goods and services produced. The

degree of _____

will have a substantial impact on the actual standard of living.

Handling of Durable Goods

20. Although consumers receive services from durable goods for more

than one year, national income accounting adds durable goods to

_____ in the year they are produced, as if the goods

were _____ in that year.

21. As incomes increase during prosperity periods, a greater quantity of durable goods are produced. Because these durable goods are not fully used in one year, the value of the _____ tends to be _____.

22. In recessions, fewer durable goods are produced, yet consumers still get service out of the items produced previously. Therefore, during periods of declining business activity, the GNP frequently _____ the standard of living.

External or Social Costs

23. When a firm produces goods and services, such internal factors as machine depreciation are considered as _____. Therefore, these costs are subtracted from GNP to obtain _____ _____ and _____.

24. There are also external or social costs in the production of goods and services. Since these external costs are _____ _____, they are not included in the total cost of the valued added that enters the GNP.

25. External costs are borne by society in the form of _____ _____.

26. The _____ and the _____ are overstated by several billion dollars annually because external costs are not subtracted from GNP.

Value of Leisure

27. Leisure time should be considered when using the GNP as a measure

    of _____ because leisure time represents

    _____ .

III. FLOW OF FUNDS

1. The GNP does not record the financial transactions of goods sold

   during the current period that were produced at _____ .

2. Because the GNP measures only _____

   _____ , it does not consider the value of

   the intermediate financial transactions which are necessary to

   produce many goods.

3. The GNP does a good job of measuring _____

   _____ but does not begin to measure _____

   _____ taking place within the

   economy in a given period.

4. In the United States, the initial _____

   _____ , published by the Federal

   Reserve, encompasses all transactions in the economy that

   occurred as a result of cash payments or _____

   _____ .

5. A similar measure in Canada is _____ .

6. List two types of transactions which are included in these
    measures that are excluded from the GNP:

    (1) _____

    (2) _____

TERMINOLOGY AND CONCEPTS INTRODUCED

intermediate products--_____

_____

end products--_____

_____

gross national product (GNP)--_____

_____

capital consumption allowances--_____

_____

net national product (NNP)--_____

_____

national income (NI)--_____

_____

personal income (PI)--_____

_____

transfer payment--_____

_____

disposable personal income (DPI)--_____

_____

discretionary income--_____

_____

GNP implicit price deflators-- _____

_____

real GNP-- _____

_____

real per capita disposable income-- _____

_____

underground (subterranean) economy-- _____

_____

flow-of-funds system of national accounts-- _____

_____

financial flow accounts-- _____

_____

SAMPLE OBJECTIVE QUESTIONS

1. The national income has a twofold definition. One way of computing
    the national income of an economy is to

    (1) add the capital consumption allowances and indirect business
        taxes to the gross national product (GNP)
    (2) add all the earnings of land, labor, capital and entrepreneurs
        in a given period
    (3) subtract indirect business taxes from the disposable personal
        income (DPI)
    (4) subtract personal interest income and government transfer
        payments from the net national product (NNP)

2. In order to compare the GNP of one year with the GNP of another year,
    economists use implicit price deflators. The GNP implicit price de-
    flators are an index that takes into account price changes and the
    changes in

    (1) level of national income
    (2) variety of products
    (3) quantity of output
    (4) quality of various products

3. The following statements can correctly be made about the make-up of Gross National Product (GNP) data:

    A. It generally takes into account only goods and services for which there have been monetary transactions

    B. It does not take into account the external or social costs arising from production

    C. It generally includes the value of durable goods in the year such goods are produced

    D. It includes transactions arising from the transfer of existing assets

    E. It makes no allowance for the value of leisure time

       (1) All of these
       (2) A, B, C and E only
       (3) B, C, D and E only
       (4) A, B and C only
       (5) A, D and E only

4. The United States flow-of-funds system of national accounts and Canadian financial flow accounts are both different from the United States and Canadian GNP accounts in that these flow accounts take into consideration

       (1) the use of already existing durable goods
       (2) changes in price levels
       (3) transfers of already existing assets
       (4) external costs resulting from the production of goods and services

ANALYSIS OF SAMPLE OBJECTIVE QUESTIONS

1. Choice (2) is the correct answer. Choices (1), (3), and (4) are all incorrect. National income (NI) could be determined by subtracting capital consumption allowances and indirect business taxes from the GNP, and then making a few other minor allowances; however, choice (1) incorrectly indicates that these amounts should be added to the GNP. NI is a larger amount than DPI; therefore, nothing could be subtracted from DPI to yield NI (3). NNP (4) is larger than NI, but the items that are subtracted from NNP to obtain NI are indirect business tax and nontax liability and business transfer payments.

2. Choice (4) is the correct answer; choices (1), (2), and (3) are all incorrect. After the GNP implicit price deflators have been used to adjust the current GNP for prices changes and some changes in the quality of various products, the result is referred to as a GNP in constant dollars, or a real GNP.

216

3. Choice (2) is the correct answer. Statements A, B, C, and E are all correct. Statement D is false because the GNP does not measure the financial transactions of goods sold during the current period that were produced at a previous time.

4. The correct answer is choice (3). Choices (1), (2), and (4) are all incorrect. Neither the GNP accounts nor the flow accounts consider the use of already existing durable goods (1) or external costs resulting from the production of goods and services (4). An evaluation of the GNP account in constant dollars considers changes in price levels (2).

REVIEW QUESTIONS

1. Specify how each of the following amounts can be determined if the GNP for a country is already known. (a) net national product (NNP), (b) national income (NI), (c) personal income (PI), (d) disposable personal income (DPI), and (e) personal savings (S).

2. Referring to statistics provided in the text, explain how failure to use GNP implicit price deflators results in distorted GNP figures.

3. Give examples of nonmonetary transactions and explain how voluntary socioeconomic organizations provide for the exchange of services in the underground economy.

13
Determinants of GNP and Economic Growth

In this chapter, you will see how a net increase in investment can cause a larger increase in the GNP and in total income. You will study the importance of the multiplier in assessing the impact of predicted economic performance. Upon completion of this chapter, you should be able to

- Explain the relationship of the multiplier to consumption and savings

- Calculate the multiplier

- Describe the cumulative action of the multiplier and the accelerator

- Use the multiplier to determine how much of an increase in investment may be necessary to reach a stage of full employment

- Discuss the impact of the rate of population increase on forecasts of economic growth

WORKING OUTLINE

Introduction

1. It is reasonable to assume that the total demand by the four

    sectors of the economy determines _____

    _____, and that the size of the GNP

    determines _____.

2. The greater the demand by the sectors of the economy, the

    greater the _____ to the factors

    of production. The less the demand, the smaller the _____.

218

3. It is primarily the demand by the four sectors of the economy that determines the _____, _____, and _____ in the economy.

I. MULTIPLIER AND ACCELERATOR

1. If each of the four sectors of a given economy demanded the same quantity of goods and services in a current year as they did in the previous year, the same _____ and the same _____ would result for the current year.

2. If one sector increases its demand, but another sector decreases its demand by a comparable amount, there will be no substantial change in _____.

3. A net gain or net loss in demand will accelerate or decelerate the level of economic activity.

The Multiplier Effect

4. The multiplier effect is the term used to refer to the fact that the total income resulting from the _____ of a given amount of money will be _____ than the actual amount of money initially spent.

5. The only limiting factor to the creation of income resulting from the respending of money will be _____
_____.

This can occur in any of the following three ways:

(1) _____ (3) _____

(2) _____

6. If at any time we withdraw money from the circular flow, that amount of money will not be available to _____

   _____.

7. _____ constitutes the biggest leakage factor from the income stream.

8. The multiplier depends on the relationship of _____ to income, or of _____ to income.

9. The multiplier is the relationship between a change in effective demand (_____ or _____ or _____) and the resulting change in income. The change in income is the result of _____, so the level of consumption has a direct influence on the size of the multiplier.

10. The more people _____ (and therefore the less they _____), the greater will be the multiplier effect.

11. Define propensity to consume. _____

    _____.

12. The stronger the propensity to consume, the _____ will be the increase in income.

13. The lower the propensity to consume, the _____ the multiplier will be.

14. Define the following terms.

    ● Average propensity to consume (APC)--_____

    _____

    ● Marginal propensity to consume (MPC)--_____

    _____

15. Although the multiplier can be calculated based on the _____,

    it is more accurate to base it on the _____.

16. Since the spending and saving habits of individuals and

    businesses change as _____, we can better tell

    what income recipients will do with their next increment of

    income by observing what they did with _____.

17. MPC will _____ as income increases.

18. As their incomes increase, the _____ and the _____

    _____ of saving by individuals will increase since

    their ability to save increases.

19. When the MPC is subtracted from 1, the result is the _____

    _____.

20. Given that K = multiplier, ΔC = the change in consumption,

    ΔY = the change in income, and 1 = the total increase in income,

    the formula for the multiplier in terms of the MPC is

    $$K = \frac{1}{\underline{\quad}} = \frac{1}{1 - MPC} = \frac{1}{MPS}$$

21. According to this equation, $\frac{\Delta C}{\Delta Y}$ is the expression

    for _____.

22. A rule of thumb for figuring the multiplier is that the

    multiplier is equal to the _____.

23. At any time, income equals _____ plus _____.

24. In order to calculate the MPC or MPS, it is necessary to observe

    two time periods and compare the _____ to the

    _____ between the two periods.

25. The multiplier is related _____ to the MPC and

    _____ to the MPS.

26. In determining the value of the multiplier, it is advisable to

    use the _____ of an individual or nation in

    order to achieve the best reflection of what is being done with

    increased incomes.

27. What is the difficult part in calculating the multiplier?

    _____ Explain your answer.

    _____

    _____

Accelerator

28. An increase in spending by _____, _____,

    or _____ initiates the multiplier effect, which

    can lead to the _____ effect.

- The increased income resulting from the multiplier effect will cause increased demand for _____.

- Businesses most likely will increase their _____ to obtain the _____ needed to produce the additional goods and services.

- New investment to increase _____ in response to _____ is known as secondary investment.

- The accelerator effect is the relationship between the spending of the increased income resulting from the multiplier on the original investment and the _____ _____.

29. Some economists feel that because of _____ _____ _____, it is impossible to measure the accelerator.

Interaction of Multiplier and Accelerator

30. The interaction of the multiplier and accelerator serves to augment each one and to boost _____ and _____.

- Through the multiplier effect, the original investment brings about increased income, which when spent brings about _____ _____.

- The multiplier effect on the _____ investment further increases income, leading to _____ _____ and so forth.

31. Define the following terms.

    ● Simple multiplier--_____

    _____

    ● Supermultiplier--_____

    _____

32. How is the supermultiplier like the accelerator? _____

    _____

33. The simple multiplier can be determined by observing the changes

    over two consecutive national income periods and comparing the

    total change in _____ to the total change in

    _____.

34. One effect of the simple multiplier is that, after the original

    investment has been spent, economic activity _____

    but at a(n) _____ rate.

35. When respending brings about induced investment, the net result

    is that income will reach a higher level than it would with

    _____.

36. The cumulative action of the multiplier and accelerator

    intensifies _____

    _____.

37. Most estimates place the length of time that elapses between the

    original investment and the respending of this money after it becomes income to others at somewhere between _____

_____, although there is no certainty regarding

this time.

38. In a given situation, if we know the multiplier, we can estimate

the amount of _____ that is needed to

reach a particular level of _____.

Production, Employment, and the Multiplier

39. State the formula for determining what amount of GNP is necessary

to maintain full employment. _____

40. If the forecast GNP is less than the full-employment GNP,

spending should be increased by any or all of the four sectors of

the economy. The amount of increased spending necessary to

bridge the gap between the forecast GNP and the full-employment

GNP depends in large part on _____.

● The amount of additional spending can be determined by dividing

the _____ into the difference between the full-

employment GNP and the forecast GNP.

41. When it is estimated that the GNP will be less than the amount

needed for a high level of employment, the administration and

agencies of the federal government may use indirect measures to

encourage _____ and _____.

42. If _____ and _____ are conser-

vative and do not respond to stimulus, the government can use

more direct measures, including _____,

in an effort to raise the level of economic activity.

II. ESTIMATING FUTURE GROWTH OF THE ECONOMY

1. Although there are several methods of obtaining a reasonable

   estimate of the future GNP, the figures produced by these methods

   are all estimates and do not purport to measure precisely the

   _____ or the _____

   for any particular year in the future.

2. Most forecasts of future growth are based largely on _____

   _____ anticipated in the future.

3. If the rate of _____ continues its

   shift downward or reverses itself, the projection of the GNP

   would have to be scaled downward or upward accordingly.

TERMINOLOGY AND CONCEPTS INTRODUCED

multiplier effect--_____

_____

multiplier--_____

_____

propensity to consume--_____

_____

average propensity to consume (APC)--_____

_____

marginal propensity to consume (MPC)--_____

_____

marginal propensity to save (MPS)--_____

_____

secondary investment--_____

_____

accelerator effect--_____

_____

simple multiplier--_____

_____

supermultiplier--_____

_____

SAMPLE OBJECTIVE QUESTIONS

1. The marginal propensity to consume is defined as the

    (1) percentage of total income spent on consumption out of any given
        level of income
    (2) relationship between the last increment of income received by
        individuals and businesses and the amount of that income spent
        on consumption
    (3) percentage of change in consumption resulting from any given
        percentage of change in total income
    (4) relationship between the total income received by individuals
        and businesses and the amount of that income spent on
        consumption

2. The following statements can correctly be made about the multiplier effect:

   A. The more money people respend, the greater will be the multiplier effect
   B. The less money people save, the greater will be the multiplier effect
   C. The multiplier is equal to the reciprocal of the marginal propensity to consume
   D. The multiplier is the relationship between a change in effective demand, investment, consumption, or government spending and the resulting change in income

      (1) A, B and C only
      (2) A, B and D only
      (3) B, C and D only
      (4) A and B nonly
      (5) A and D only

3. The concept of "multiplier" is important in explaining economic activity. In any given economy, the multiplier is equal to

   (1) $\dfrac{\text{(the marginal propensity to consume)}}{\text{(the marginal propensity to save)}}$

   (2) $\dfrac{1}{\text{(the marginal propensity to consume)}}$

   (3) $\dfrac{1}{\text{(the marginal propensity to save)}}$

   (4) $\dfrac{\text{(the marginal propensity to save)}-}{\text{(the marginal propensity to consume)}}$

4. The term "accelerator effect" refers to the economic concept that

   (1) the spending of increased income resulting from the multiplier leads to secondary or induced investment
   (2) individuals tend to save a higher proportion of earnings as their incomes increase
   (3) inflationary wages lead to higher taxes and result in subsequent demands for yet higher wages
   (4) workers' demand for higher earnings to match price increases leads to higher costs, and still higher prices

ANALYSIS OF SAMPLE OBJECTIVE QUESTIONS

1. Choice (2) is the correct answer. Choices (1), (3) and (4) are all similar to the definition of the marginal propensity to consume (MPC), but only choice (2) contains the actual definition.

2. The correct answer is choice (2). Statements A, B, and D are all correct. Statement C is false because the multiplier is equal to the reciprocal of the marginal propensity to save.

3. Choice (3) is the correct answer, and choices (1), (2), and (4) are all incorrect. As stated above, the multiplier is equal to the reciprocal of the marginal propensity to save. In mathematical notation, the reciprocal of the marginal propensity to save is represented as the fraction shown in choice (3).

4. Choice (1) is the correct answer. Choices (2), (3), and (4) are all incorrect because none of them deal with the concepts of investment and the multiplier, which are the basis of the accelerator effect.

REVIEW QUESTIONS

1. Assuming that there is a net increase in investment of $30 billion and that the MPS equals .33, answer the following questions.

   (a) What is the multiplier? **(A)**
   (b) How much will gross income increase as a result of this net increase in investment? **(A)**
   (c) When the respending process is complete, how much will savings have increased as a result of this net increase in investment? **(A)**
   (d) The net increase in investment and the respending process will cause how much increased spending? **(A)**

2. Explain why the general tendency in any economy is for the MPC to decrease as real income increases, provided other things remain unchanged. Why is this general tendency not true in every case?

3. What are some of the problems encountered in attempting to distinguish original investment from secondary investment?

4. Assume that the normally employed labor force in a given year is 102 million, the average working hours per person per year are 2,000, and the productivity per work-hour is $15. Then, assume that the full-employment GNP is $3,100 billion and the multiplier is 4.

   (a) What is the potential GNP? **(A)**
   (b) What is the difference between the potential and the full-employment GNP? **(A)**
   (c) How much must net investment increase in order to maintain full employment? **(A)**

ANSWERS TO SELECTED REVIEW QUESTIONS

1. (a) $k = \dfrac{1}{MPS} = \dfrac{1}{.33} = $ approximately 3

    (b) net increase in investment x multiplier = increase in gross income;
    $30 billion x 3 = $90 billion

    (c) $30 billion (The process of receiving and respending income will continue until the original amount of money is all held in savings by various individuals.)

    (d) Increase in gross income minus Increase in savings = Increase in spending; $90 billion - $30 billion = $60 billion

4. (a) Labor force x Hours per Worker x Output per Work-Hour = Potential GNP
    102 million x 2,000 x $15 = $3,060 billion

    (b) $3,100 billion - $3,060 billion = $40 billion
    (c) $40 billion ÷ 4 = $10 billion

14

Macroeconomic Analysis

OBJECTIVES

In this chapter, you will study some of the principles and doctrines of classical economics. You will be introduced to three theories of macroeconomic analysis: income-expenditure analysis, the theory of rational expectations, and supply-side economics. Upon completion of this chapter, you should be able to

- Identify the ways in which the income-expenditure analysis deviates from the classical tradition

- State the purpose of the income expenditure theory

- Explain the importance of the relationship between the marginal efficiency on capital and the rate of interest

- Describe the impact on the economy of changes in various elements of the income-expenditure theory

- Give examples of behavior of individuals and firms that can neutralize government economic stabilization measures

- Discuss the differences between supply-side economics and the income-expenditure analysis

WORKING OUTLINE

Introduction

1. Macroeconomic analysis deals with the aggregates of economics,

   such as _____, _____,

   and _____.

2. Who was primarily responsible for the early development of the income-expenditure analysis of the of the economy? _____

_____

3. Modern monetary, fiscal, and psychological policies are difficult to understand without a knowledge of the principles of the income-expenditure analysis, which is often referred to today as

_____.

4. The theory of rational expectations arose in the 1960s and the 1970s in response to what were perceived as shortcomings in

_____.

5. Based largely on the _____ of the business cycle, the theory of rational expectations holds that individuals and firms in the economy react according to their _____

_____, and

especially according to their _____

_____.

6. According to the theory of rational expectations, the optimism or pessimism of individuals and firms may so strongly influence their behavior that _____

_____.

7. Supply-side economics, which emerged about the same time that the theory of rational expectations gained popularity, focuses on the impact on the total supply of goods and services which results

from government policies affecting _____, _____, _____, and _____.

I. INCOME-EXPENDITURE ANALYSIS AND CLASSICAL TRADITION

1. The development of income-expenditure analysis involved a breaking away from the principles and doctrines of classical economics.

Full Employment

2. What assumption is of greatest importance to the classical tradition? _____

    _____

3. According to the classical theory, the economy operates on the basis of _____ and _____.

4. Competition, the _____ of the free economy, is an important factor in maintaining or moving the economy toward full employment.

5. Competition will force prices _____ to ensure that

    _____.

6. Competition will ensure that all savings are _____, by forcing the interest rate down until _____

    _____

    _____.

7. Because of competition, unemployment for extended periods is _____ if not _____.

● If workers are unemployed, it is assumed that they will compete

  for jobs by _____

  _____.

● As a result of this competition, wages will be _____

  _____.

● As wage rates _____, it becomes profitable for

  the entrepreneurs to _____.

8. Economists of the classical tradition believe that temporary
   deviations of the economy away from full employment are caused
   primarily by the following three factors:

   (1) _____ (3) _____

   (2) _____

Income Equals Expenditures

9. What do adherents of classical theory maintain is the primary

   purpose of money? _____

10. According to classical theorists all income will be spent. In
    what three ways will people spend their income?

    (1) _____ (3) _____

    (2) _____

11. If any money is saved, classical theorist believe it will be

    borrowed by others and spent in various ways, especially for

    _____.

12. Thus, any decrease in _____ will be

    offset by an increase in _____.

13. Fluctuations in the interest rate will ensure that _____

    _____ .

Supply Creates Demand

14. List three assumptions of Say's law.

    (1) _____

    (2) _____

    (3) _____

15. In contrast, the income-expenditure analysis contends that

    purchasing power does not automatically _____

    _____ . Therefore,

    total demand for goods and services may be less than the

    _____ . Then, there would be no incentive to _____

    _____ or to _____ .

16. According to the income-expenditure analysis, a problem arises in

    an economy when individuals substitute a desire for savings

    in place of _____ , and these

    savings are not offset by _____ .

    ● As goods are produced, supply is created, which also creates

      _____ , but some of the _____

    may be held in idle balances.

17. The income-expenditure analysis contends that the economy will

    maintain equilibrium only when _____ .

II. INCOME-EXPENDITURE ANALYSIS

1. According to the income-expenditure analysis, as output _____ ,
    income increases; as income increases, _____ increases,
    but at a lesser rate.

2. Since the MPS _____ as income increases, an
    ever-increasing amount of investment is needed to fill the gap
    between _____ and _____ if
    all the goods produced are to be moved off the market.

3. According to the income-expenditure analysis, the following
    equations are true when the economy is at equilibrium:

    ● Planned investment = _____

    ● Investment = _____ - _____ **(A)**

    ● Total spending = _____

    ● Effective demand = _____

4. Investment becomes the important determinant for the following
    three factors:

    (1) _____   (3) _____

    (2) _____

5. Since the consumption function is relatively stable in the short
    run, the level of employment cannot be increased without an
    increase in _____ . The higher the level of
    _____ , however, the less the _____
    required to obtain any given level of employment.

6. The economy can become stabilized at an undesirable level of employment because of _____.

   • If this occurs, income-expenditure theory promotes the adoption of _____

   designed to encourage _____ and _____.

   • Such measures should raise the level of _____ and _____.

   • If the attempt to raise the level of effective demand through _____ and _____ is un-

   successful, _____ can be utilized

   in order to bring the economy to a higher level of employment.

Purpose of Theory

7. What is the ultimate purpose of the income-expenditure theory?

   _____

   _____

8. Income-expenditure analysis seeks a practical explanation to the _____, in the hope

   of discovering those variables that cause changes in the

   _____. Once those variables are

   found, pressure can then be applied to them to _____

   _____.

Marginal Efficiency of Capital and Rate of Interest

9. According to the income-expenditure analysis, the following relationships exist between the factors of the economy:

● Effective demand is determined by _____

_____ and _____.

● Effective demand determines the following three factors:

(1) _____ (3) _____

(2) _____

● Consumption is determined by _____ and

_____.

● If the propensity to consume remains stable, _____

_____, _____, and _____

will be determined by the amount of investment.

10. Investment is dependent upon the marginal efficiency of capital

(<u>MEC</u>) and the _____ (_____).

11. According to the income-expenditure analysis, the _____

is the active factor in determining whether businesses are going

to borrow and invest; the _____ is the passive factor.

● If the <u>MEC</u> is high compared to the <u>RI</u>, _____

_____.

● If the <u>MEC</u> is low compared to the RI, _____

_____.

12. The following occurrences can enhance the <u>MEC</u>:

● An increase in _____

● A decrease in _____

13. The MEC is _____ and subject to _____;

    therefore, it can easily take into account variations in invest-

    ment.

14. It is the relationship between MEC and RI that causes _____,

    _____, or _____ in the

    economy.

15. Whenever MEC > RI, there will be an expansion in business
    activity. As expansion takes place, however, forces will bring
    the MEC and the RI into balance.

    ● The MEC will decline when sales begin to _____

      and the price level _____ or begins to decline.

    ● The increased demand for _____ and the pressure

      on _____, caused by the expansion,

      will force the RI upward.

16. Whenever MEC = RI, there will be a stable flow of economic
    activity.

    ● At this point, there is no further incentive for business to

      _____ and _____.

    ● If this point does not correspond to the point of full employ-

      ment, or at least to a high level of employment, monetary

      measures can be used in an attempt to _____

      _____.

17. Whenever MEC < RI, the level of economic activity will begin to
    fall. As this contraction takes place, forces will bring the
    MEC and the RI into balance again.

    ● There will be a decrease of investment in the economy, and a

      decrease in _____.

239

- In turn, _____, _____, and

  _____ will further decline.

- The RI will begin to decline, and the MEC will eventually pick
  up.

18. According to the income-expenditure theory, _____

    is a period in which the RI exceeds the MEC.

19. In balancing the MEC and the RI, the _____ is the more important

    and active factor, but it is easier to make artificial

    adjustments in the _____ when a bolstering of the

    economy through governmental policies is desired.

Determinants of the Rate of Interest

20. Why is it important to know the determinants of RI?

    _____

    _____

21. According to the income-expenditure analysis, the RI is dependent

    upon the strength of _____ compared

    to the _____ in the economy.

- Define liquidity preference. _____

  _____

- Liquidity may be desired for any of the following three
  reasons:

    (1) _____ (3) _____

    (2) _____

22. The explanation for the transaction motive is that individuals

    and firms save money for _____.

23. The explanation for the precautionary motive is that individuals and firms save in order to accumulate funds for _____, for _____, and for _____.

24. The rationale behind the speculative motive is that individuals and firms hold money to take advantage of _____ _____.

25. The speculative motive is more _____ and subject to sharper changes than either the transaction or precautionary motives and has a substantial effect on RI.

    ● When it is anticipated that business activity is going to be good, the demand for money for speculative purposes will be great and the RI will _____.

    ● When the demand for speculative funds decreases, the RI will _____.

26. Although the liquidity preference will vary among individuals and firms, it generally will _____ when prices are rising and _____ when prices are declining.

27. The RI will vary directly with the liquidity preference because the stronger the liquidity preference, _____ _____ _____.

28. The greater the amount of money existing in the economy compared to the liquidity preference, the _____ the RI.

241

29. Assume that individuals and firms desire to hold a certain amount of liquid funds.

● What will happen if the money supply is increased?

_____

_____

● What will happen if the quantity of money is decreased?

_____

_____

III. RECAP OF INCOME-EXPENDITURE ANALYSIS

1. Each of the phrases in the left-hand column below is the first half of a statement expressing the relationship between various elements of the income-expenditure theory. In the blank beside each partial statement, write the letter identifying the phrase in the right-hand column that accurately completes that statement.

____(1) Consumption depends on

____(2) The RI depends upon

____(3) Investment is determined by

____(4) Effective demand is made up of

____(5) Liquidity preference depends on

____(6) Output, income, and employment depend on

____(7) The MEC is dependent upon

a. Consumption, investment, and government spending

b. Effective demand

c. Liquidity preference compared to the quantity of money

d. The MEC compared to the RI

e. Profit expectation compared to the cost of capital assets

f. The size of income and the propensity to consume

g. The strength of the trans-actions, precautionary, and speculative motives for saving

242

2. The propensity to consume is relatively stable; therefore, assuming nominal government spending to have _____ _____, changes in employment will result primarily from changes in _____.

3. In the absence of sufficient _____ and _____, changes in government spending can be used to influence the level of output, income, and employment.

4. In income-expenditure analysis, the three strategic variables are

   (1) _____ (3) _____

   (2) _____

5. The income-expenditure analysis has been criticized because in the long run it will require larger and larger amounts of government spending. State three flaws in this argument.

   (1) _____

   (2) _____

   (3) _____

6. Present two other criticisms of income-expenditure analysis.

   (1) _____

   _____

   (2) _____

   _____

IV. THE THEORY OF RATIONAL EXPECTATIONS

1. With the changing economic conditions of the 1970s, it became
    apparent that policies and measures based on income-expenditure
    analysis were not always successful in the attempt to achieve and
    maintain _____, _____,
    and _____.

2. At this time, the theory of rational expectations emerged.

3. This theory is largely a modification of the _____
    theory of the _____.

    ● According to this _____ theory, when
      business investors and consumers think that economic conditions
      are going to be good, their actions will be such that _____
      _____.

    ● When the outlook of business investors and consumers is
      pessimistic, their actions will be such that _____
      _____.

    ● The actions of business investors and consumers are _____
      _____ since they tend to _____
      _____ movements of business activity.

4. The theory of rational expectations goes beyond the psychological
    theory by making the following two assumptions:

    (1) _____
        _____

    (2) _____
        _____

* * * * * *

Statements 5 through 8 below describe the behavior of business investors or consumers in various situations. Complete each statement so that it illustrates behavior in accordance with the theory of rational expectations.

5. In an expanding economy with rising prices, business investors who expect the central bank to respond with tighter money and higher interest rates may borrow and invest _____ _____, thus aggravating the inflationary situation.

6. Anticipating the implementation of an incomes policy, a firm may seek _____ and grant _____.

7. In an expanding economy with upward price pressures, consumers may anticipate the imposition of credit restrictions or an increase in home mortgage rates and may accelerate _____ _____ or hasten _____.

8. During the early stages of a recession, business leaders may anticipate a lowering of the discount and prime interest rates and the adoption of tax credits or accelerated depreciation on new investment. In response to these beliefs, investors may decide to postpone the purchase of equipment or the construction of new buildings until _____ _____.

* * * * * *

245

9. In each of the instances described above, the actions of consumers and firms diminished the impact of government economic policies.

10. Assume that the economic atmosphere is one in which inflation is expected to continue unabated. In such an atmosphere:

   • Consumers may continue to buy in spite of _____

   _____ and _____ .

   • Businesses may invest more regardless of _____ ,

   _____ , and _____ .

   • Workers may demand _____ to offset the impact

   of inflation on their purchasing power.

   • Lenders may require _____

   to avoid a decline in real estate rates.

V. SUPPLY-SIDE ECONOMICS

1. Define supply-side economics. _____

   _____

   _____

2. Supply-side policies are a combination of _____ ,

   _____ , _____ , and _____

   measures designed to encourage increases in saving, investment,

   and work effort in order to bring about _____ ,

   _____ , and _____ ,

   via the effect of such increases on total supply.

Tax Rate and Output

3. Supply-side advocates blame many of the United States' economic problems of the 1970s on _____ and

   _____ .

4. According to supply-siders, there is an optimum tax rate that maximizes output, and a reduction in the _____ in the United States would increase production and _____ .

5. Taxes, particularly _____ , affect the supply of labor utilized.

   - If there were no payroll tax, the wage received by workers would be equal to _____ .

   - The presence of payroll taxes causes a smaller quantity of labor to be demanded because the cost of employing workers is more than the _____ .

   - The presence of payroll taxes causes the workers' take-home pay to be less, so there is a smaller _____ .

6. Payroll taxes act as a labor tax wedge between _____

   _____ and _____

   _____ .

7. According to many supply-side advocates, a(n) _____ in tax rates is necessary to bring about an increase in the

   _____ and the _____

   in order to increase employment or reduce unemployment.

8. According to some supply-siders, an investment tax wedge exists
   between the _____ and the _____
   in the market for loanable funds.

9. The investment tax wedge exists because the lender has to pay tax
   on _____ and the borrower has to
   pay tax on _____
   _____.

10. Supply-side advocates believe that a lowering of tax rates will
    stimulate investment by _____
    _____.

11. Supply-siders believe that a reduction in tax rates will
    encourage savings by _____
    _____.

12. Supply-siders feel that, because of _____,
    many funds today are diverted into tax-sheltered investments.
    • They feel that tax-sheltered investments are less productive
      than _____.
    • They maintain that lower tax rates will encourage _____
      _____ which, in turn, will increase
      _____, _____, and tax
      receipts.

13. The graph most often associated with supply-side economics is the
    _____.

14. Supply-side advocates claim that much of the benefit from tax reductions can be obtained without _____

    _____.

15. According to the Laffer curve, there are two points at which tax revenues are zero. Describe these points.

    (1) _____

    (2) _____

16. The Laffer curve shows that at some optimum rate (not necessarily a _____ percent tax rate), revenues will be maximized.

17. Tax rates that exceed the optimum rates are in the _____

    _____ and will cause the tax revenues to decline.

18. Another complexity is the fact that both Canada and the United States have varying tax _____ and numerous tax_____,

    each with different _____.

Government Spending and Regulation

19. Supply-siders believe that government spending is less _____

    _____ than spending by the private sector.

20. They suggest a reduction in government spending to permit tax reduction. The consequent increase in real income to the private sector will be spent more _____ as the increased income encourages _____, stimulates _____,

    and motivates _____.

21. Supply-siders recommend deregulation, which is the _____

_____, in order

to increase productivity, total output, employment, and income.

Need for a Stable Money Supply

22. Supply-side advocates recognize a need for a stable money supply

in order to provide _____

_____.

23. Supply-siders recommend a return to a gold standard in light of

_____ and _____

_____

_____.

Criticisms of Supply-Side Proposals

24. Supply-side advocates and their critics disagree over the effects
of a tax cut on interest income, investment income, and wage and
salary income.

25. According to supply-siders, what would be the effect of an

increase in the after-tax return on savings, investment, and

worker effort? _____

_____

- Higher after-tax returns for savings increase the opportunity

  cost of _____.

- The higher opportunity cost induces individuals to choose more

  savings over more _____, and to opt for more

  work instead of more _____.

● The choice of more savings or more work in response a(n) _____ is known as the _____.

26. Critics note that some individuals have a(n) _____ that they desire to obtain from their savings or work effort.

   ● If the after-tax income on savings and work effort is increased such an individual may decided that _____

   _____

   _____.

   ● The choice of fewer savings or less _____ in response to a(n) _____ is called the income effect.

27. At the present time, there is no strong empirical evidence that shows to what extent the substitution effect is greater or less than the income effect.

28. Concerning the growth of the tax base illustrated in the Laffer curve, supply-siders claim that tax reductions could generate sufficient increases in _____, and therefore, the _____, to make up for the loss of revenue resulting from the decrease in _____.

29. Critics feel that the increase in tax revenue from the increase in tax base most likely will not offset the _____

   _____.

30. Supply-side advocates and their critics disagree over the effectiveness of government spending.

● The supply-side viewpoint is that government spending is

_____ than spending by the private

sector.

● Critics state that the multiplier effect of government spending

is greater than that of the private sector because _____

_____.

● The issue is further complicated when the _____

of government spending are compared with those of private

sector spending.

31. Supply-side proposals are not designed as short-run _____

_____. Rather, they are long-run proposals

designed to _____

_____.

32. Although supply-side economics probably will not replace
Keynesian income-expenditure economics, in the future the governments of Canada and the United States are likely to consider both
the supply side and the income-expenditure, or demand-side,
effects before implementing economic policies and measures.

SELECTED ANSWERS TO WORKING OUTLINE

II. INCOME-EXPENDITURE ANALYSIS

3.   Investment = <u>output</u> - <u>consumption</u>

TERMINOLOGY AND CONCEPTS INTRODUCED

Rate of interest (<u>RI</u>)--_____

_____

marginal efficiency of capital (<u>MEC</u>)--_____

_____

disinvest--_____

_____

liquidity preference--_____

_____

transactions motive--_____

_____

precautionary motive--_____

_____

speculative motive--_____

_____

supply-side economics--_____

_____

labor tax wedge--_____

_____

investment tax wedge--_____

_____

Laffer curve--_____

_____

prohibitive range--_____

_____

substitution effect--_____

_____

income effect--_____

_____

SAMPLE OBJECTIVE QUESTIONS

1. According to classical economic theory, if the economy is at less than full employment

   (1) increased government spending is necessary to obtain full employment
   (2) inflationary forces will tend to accelerate
   (3) competition in the labor market moves the economy to full employment
   (4) an increase in the rate of interest is necessary to obtain full employment

2. The following statements can correctly be made about the basic theories and purposes of income-expenditure analysis in economics:

   A. The ultimate purpose of income-expenditure theory is to explain what determines the level of employment in the economy and to show the causes of unemployment
   B. The marginal propensity to consume increases as the real income of individuals increases
   C. Changes in the level of government spending can be used to influence the levels of output, income and employment
   D. The economy is in equilibrium at a point where investment fills completely the gap between output and consumption

      (1) All of these
      (2) A, B and C only
      (3) A, C and D only
      (4) B and D only
      (5) C and D only

3. According to the income-expenditure analysis, the relationship between the strength of the desire to hold assets in the form of cash and the quantity of money in the economy determines the

   (1) rate of interest on loans
   (2) rate of return on investments
   (3) level of employment in the economy
   (4) price levels in an economy

4. According to critics of supply-side economics, the income effect is the

   (1) choice of fewer savings or less work in response to a tax cut
   (2) desire to convert cash into assets when the value of money is low
   (3) choice of more savings or more work in response to a tax cut
   (4) desire to hold assets in the form of cash when the value of money is high

254

ANALYSIS OF SAMPLE OBJECTIVE QUESTIONS

1. Choice (3) is the correct answer. Choices (1), (2), and (4) are all incorrect. According to classical economic theory, if workers are unemployed, they will compete for jobs by offering to work for lower wages. As wage rates decline, entrepreneurs will hire more workers, bringing the economy to full employment. Therefore, there need not be increased government spending (1) or an increase in interest rates (4) to bring the economy to full employment. Classical economists believe that competition during period of less than full employment will force prices downward to ensure that all goods are moved off the market; therefore, there will not be an acceleration of inflationary forces (2).

2. The correct answer is choice (3). Statements A, C, and D are all correct. Statement B is false because the marginal propensity to save increases as real income increases. Since

$$\text{Marginal Propensity to Save} + \text{Marginal Propensity to Consume} = 1$$

an increase in the marginal propensity to save will correspond to a decrease in the marginal propensity to consume. Therefore, as the real income of individuals increases, the marginal propensity to consume decreases.

3. The correct answer is choice (1). Choices (2), (3), and (4) are all incorrect. According to the income-expenditure analysis, the rate of interest (RI) is dependent upon the strength of liquidity preference compared to the quantity of money in the economy.

4. Choice (1) is the correct answer. Choice (2) identifies a decreased liquidity preference. Choice (3) defines the substitution effect, and choice (4) describes a strong liquidity preference.

REVIEW QUESTIONS

1. According to classical tradition, what role does competition play in maintaining or moving the economy toward full employment?

2. According to advocates of the income-expenditure analysis, what role should government action play in bolstering the economy?

3. What is disinvestment and when is it likely to occur?

4. Give examples of each of the three motives for desiring liquidity.

5. In what ways is the theory of rational expectations different from the psychological theory of the business cycle?

15
Macroeconomic Policies

OBJECTIVES

In this chapter, you will study the economic policies employed in Canada and the United States to stabilize economic activity by alleviating unemployment, combating inflation, or reducing total spending. The chapter concludes with an introduction to the councils in the United States and Canada that assist in the formulation of macroeconomic policies. Upon completion of this chapter, you should be able to

- Explain the importance of those economic institutions or practices that serve as built-in stabilizers for the economy

- Contrast the three methods available to finance government spending

- Describe the impact of the balanced budget multiplier effect

- Discuss the relative merits of using government spending to make direct monetary payments to the unemployed and the poor or to finance major public works projects

- Explain how government surplus produces a reduction in total spending

- Describe the Phillips curve

- Identify the dilemma economists face when attempting to deal with stagflation or slumpflation

WORKING OUTLINE

I. EXPANSIONARY POLICIES

1. Since _____ and _____ can come

    into equilibrium at a position of less than _____,

    the economy can stabilize at an unemployment level and can remain

    there for some period of time.

2. The income-expenditure analysis provides the basis for developing

    policies and measures designed to move the economy into _____

    _____ at _____.

II. POLICIES TO ALLEVIATE UNEMPLOYMENT

1. List four hardships that often accompany high levels of unemploy-
    ment.

    (1) _____ (3) _____

    (2) _____ (4) _____

2. What three general policies can be developed to promote maximum
    income with full employment?

    (1) _____

    (2) _____

    (3) _____

Built-In Stabilizers

3. A number of economic institutions or practices in Canada or the
    United States tend to serve as built-in stabilizers for the
    economy.

4. List six examples of built-in stabilizers.

    (1) _____ (4) _____

    (2) _____ (5) _____

    (3) _____ (6) _____

5. Define the following terms:

    ● Fiscal drag-- _____

    ● Fiscal stimulus-- _____

Monetary Policy

6. Whenever a recession occurs, it is important that bank credit be

    easier to obtain, but only _____.

7. Describe four methods that the central bank can use to make
    easier credit available.

    (1) _____

    _____

    (2) _____

    _____

    (3) _____

    _____

    (4) _____

    _____

8. What factors would the central bank consider in deciding whether

    to use one or more of these methods? _____

    _____

    _____

9. Credit can be made more easily obtainable, but there is no

    certainty that _____

10. The primary objectives of monetary policy are _____

    _____ and _____.

11. Because of the limitations of monetary policy, regulation of
    the money supply can only serve as a partial corrective to
    instability.

12. The fiscal powers of the government are probably more effective

    for the task of _____,

    especially during a period of _____.

Discretionary Fiscal Policy

13. Government revenues and expenditures may be adjusted in a manner

    that will _____ during a recession,

    _____ when the economy is overheating,

    and _____ in the long run.

14. List the three ways of financing government spending.

    (1) _____ (3) _____

    (2) _____

15. If taxation is used to finance government spending, caution must

    be exercised not to tax funds that _____

    _____.

    ● If such spendable funds are taxed, then total effective demand

      _____ and no increase in employment

    results.

    ● If only idle funds are taxed, government taxation and spending

      lead to an increase in total _____

      via the _____.

16. Generally, any tax structure absorbs _____ and

    _____ funds to some significant degree.

17. Borrowing is a more desirable method of raising funds for government spending when the purpose of spending the funds is to

_____.

18. The source of borrowing--_____, _____, or

_____--will have a direct bearing on the effect, but the total effect will depend on whether or not the government borrows idle funds.

- If the government, through the sale of bonds to individuals and businesses, borrows spendable funds, the effect of government spending will be negated because total effective demand will show no _____.

- If, however, the individuals and businesses use idle funds to purchase the government bonds, there will be a net increase in effective demand when _____.

19. Since some individuals and businesses may _____

_____,

bank borrowing is usually recognized as the most feasible method to bring about _____.

20. Bank borrowing is not likely to have an adverse effect on the

_____ by individuals and firms.

21. Describe the process whereby the government can borrow funds in excess of the actual savings, without hampering consumption or investment spending. _____

_____

22. To the extent that government spending is financed by the

    creation of bank credit, there is an increase in the _____

    _____ as well as an increase in the total effective

    demand.

23. The government can finance its increased spending without having

    to _____ by printing additional money.

24. It is often difficult to increase the amount of currency unless

    the government can increase _____.

25. Although printing more money for government spending has not been
    a very acceptable method of bolstering the economy, some
    economists feel the government should use such printed money.
    State the primary argument advanced by these economists.

26. One alternative suggested by the economists who favor the use of

    printed money is the use of interest-free financing. With this

    method, the federal treasury would sell _____

    to the central bank, and the central bank in turn would create

    _____ for the government.

Methods of Increasing Government Spending

27. What are the three methods whereby government spending can be

    used to increase the level of employment?

    (1) _____ (3) _____

    (2) _____

28. If the government increases its spending and holds taxes

constant, there is a(n) _____ in the

amount of money spent by the government.

● The government will have to borrow money to fund its additional
   expenditures.

● This method is beneficial insofar as the government can easily

   maintain close control over _____

   _____ .

29. If the government follows the "tax remission" plan, which

involves holding government spending constant and _____ ,

a(n) _____ is likely to result.

● The government will be short of needed funds and will be forced
   to borrow.

30. With this method, the government is not _____ ,

but it is assumed that the recipients of the tax remission will

spend the money either for _____ or _____ .

● To the extent that the recipients may not _____

   _____ , the effect of using this method to increase

   employment is lessened.

● The direction of their _____ may also be

   less effective.

31. This method is politically popular and is favored by the

advocates of _____ .

32. If the government increases its spending and increases taxes

_____ , it can maintain a balanced budget.

262

- The effectiveness of this method is limited by the fact that, in raising taxes, the government may _____

_____.

- The whole success of this program depends on _____

_____.

33. Since most tax measures force consumers and investors to _____

_____, this method

usually requires a larger amount of government spending than do

the other two methods to raise the level of employment by a given

amount.

- What is the balanced budget multiplier effect? _____

_____

_____

- If the MPS for the economy as a whole is one half, what level
  must government spending and taxation reach to cause a $20
  billion net increase in effective demand, exclusive of the
  multiplier and accelerator effect? **(A)**

34. Because of its limitations, this method is practicable only for

_____, or if _____

_____.

Direction of Emergency Government Spending

35. Direct monetary payments can be made to the unemployed and the
     poor. List one advantage and one disadvantage of this method.

- Advantage--_____

- Disadvantage--_____

36. If an individual is given a direct payment, the bulk of the payment is spent for _____.

37. The money paid as direct payments does not have the beneficial ripple effects of money paid for major public works projects.

38. The following statements describe some of the benefits of a major public work:

    ● It necessitates the use of _____

    and the production of _____.

    ● It stimulates _____.

    ● It results in payments to many types of workers, who in turn purchase consumer goods that other workers are employed to produce.

    ● It generates more secondary and tertiary employment than do direct payments.

    ● It creates a greater multiplier effect than do direct payments.

    ● It results in something to show for the spending and production efforts.

39. The income-expenditure approach makes use of the _____ multiplier and the _____ multiplier to show the net result of an increase in _____.

40. The employment multiplier, _____, is the ratio of the total increase in employment, _____ to the original increase of employment, _____. Write the formula for the employment multiplier in the space below.

    _____

41. The employment multiplier may or may not be equal to the

    _____.

42. Once the employment multiplier is known, it can be determined rather easily what amount of employment on public works will be necessary to raise the total level of employment a desired amount.

- Assume an employment multiplier of 2 and a current level of 50 million employed. If the government desires to raise the level of employment to 58 million, how many workers must be hired in public works? **(A)**

- The higher the employment multiplier, the easier it is to bring

    about _____ through

    public works.

43. Emergency spending can be used to fill the gap between output

    and _____ whenever consumption and _____

    _____ are insufficient to bring about a high level

    of employment. However, attaining the objective of a high level

    of employment may require _____

    _____.

III. ANTI-INFLATIONARY POLICIES

1. The income-expenditure analysis is often referred to as _____

    _____ because it emerged during the 1930s and

    consequently placed primary emphasis on the _____.

2. The income-expenditure approach can also be used to analyze

    _____ and formulate _____.

3. According to the income-expenditure approach, inflation will

    occur at the full-employment level during any period in which the

    _____ exceeds the _____.

● Such a period will occur when _____ and

_____ are more than sufficient to fill

the gap between consumption and total output.

● Demand-pull inflation will exist when current demand exceeds

_____ so that

competitive bidding by spenders will _____.

● List three other types of inflation that may exist during this
period.

(1) _____   (3) _____

(2) _____

4. Although income-expenditure analysis provides an explanation of

the causes and cures of _____ and _____

_____ at full employment, it does not provide

an adequate framework for analyzing the causes of and cures for

_____.

5. List three possible causes of demand-pull inflation.

(1) _____   (3) _____

(2) _____

6. There are two alternative means of combating demand-pull
inflation.

● The first and best is to _____

_____, but

this is not always feasible in a(n) _____

in the short run.

● The second alternative is to _____

_____.

IV. MEASURES TO REDUCE TOTAL SPENDING

1. In order to reduce total spending in the economy, spending can be reduced in the following three areas:

   (1) _____ (3) _____

   (2) _____

Built in Stabilizers

2. Cite three examples of how built-in stabilizers can act as a deterrent to inflation.

   (1) _____

   _____

   (2) _____

   _____

   (3) _____

   _____

Monetary Policy

3. Measures designed to _____

   and/or _____ tend to

   discourage investment.

4. A reduction in investment lowers the _____.

5. Investment could be reduced to a point where it just fills the

   gap between the combined effective demand of _____

267

(including _____) and _____

_____ at full employment

6. What is one advantage in using monetary policy to combat
   inflation? _____

   _____

7. The anti-inflationary effects of a rise in the interest rate can
   be offset by _____.

8. According to the income-expenditure analysis, in the absence of
   direct regulations, there is little that can be done about
   controlling _____. Therefore, the government
   must rely heavily on _____
   and _____ to
   combat inflation through its monetary policy.

Other Measures

9. The government may discourage investment and consumption by imposing credit restraints on both commercial and consumer loans.
   Cite three examples of this tactic.

   (1) _____

   (2) _____

   (3) _____

10. What are two other measures the government can use to discourage
    investment and consumption?

    (1) _____

    (2) _____

Government Surplus

11. During an inflationary period, total spending may be reduced in the economy by using policies opposite to those for increasing spending during a depression:

    ● The government can limit its spending to _____.

    ● The government can operate with _____, so that it receives more in taxes than it spends. This will tend to reduce the _____ in the economy.

    ● The government should endeavor to tax _____ rather than _____.

12. What are the two ways in which government can combat inflation by building a surplus?

    (1) _____

    (2) _____

13. What other method can the government use to combat inflation?

    _____

14. If taxes are held constant and government spending is decreased in order to combat inflation, the policy will be more effective if spending is decreased in those areas that _____ _____.

15. Cite one advantage and one disadvantage of this method.

    ● Advantage--_____

    ● Disadvantage--_____

16. If higher taxes are used to combat inflation, taxes should be

    increased in such a manner that _____

    _____.

17. A combination of higher taxes and decreased government spending
    is doubly effective in combating inflation.

18. The combination of lower taxes and lower government spending can

    be deflationary if taxes are decreased in those areas where

    _____.

    ● This method will reduce total spending by _____,

      provided those who receive the tax reduction _____

      _____.

    ● Cite two problems with this method.

      (1) _____

      _____

      (2) _____

      _____

19. To reduce effective demand, it is beneficial for a government to

    establish a surplus by absorbing the _____

    _____.

20. Through taxation, the government can reduce the total effective

    demand to a point where _____, and

    thus remove or lessen _____.

21. Government spending can be reduced so that the combination of

    _____ and _____ will

just equal the gap between consumption and output at full

employment.

22. An increase in taxes can reduce the amount of _____

and _____ so that government spending fits into the

gap between total private effective demand and _____ ,

thus eliminating the inflation gap.

23. If the government does use a surplus budget for the purpose of
combating inflation, it is essential that the government maintain
the surplus. What other two actions could be taken, and how
would each of these negate the desired anti-inflationary effect
of surplus.

1. _____

_____

2. _____

_____

Borrowing

24. Government bond drives can reduce total effective demand,

provided firms and individuals _____

_____

_____.

25. How do anti-inflationary bond drives differ from bond drives

during a depression? _____

_____

_____

V. THE TRADE-OFF BETWEEN UNEMPLOYMENT AND INFLATION

1. Once the economy is at full employment, it is difficult to ride the crest of the economy at the point where unemployment is _____ and the price level is _____.

2. It appears that there is a trade-off between increased _____ _____ and an increase in _____.

3. British economist A.W. Phillips plotted this trade-off on what is known as a Phillips curve.

   ● He concluded that the money wage level would stabilize with a

   _____.

4. Beginning in the 1960s, United States economists began to apply the Phillips curves to changes in _____ in relation to _____.

5. State two reasons why any interpretation of Phillips curves must be made cautiously.

   (1) _____

   (2) _____

6. In light of recent data, some analysts have challenged the Phillips curve and its relationship between unemployment and price-level changes. However, it should be remembered that the Phillips curve was originally designed to measure the relationship between unemployment and _____ not _____, _____, or _____.

Stagflation--A Special Problem

7. Define the following terms:

    ● Stagflation--_____

       _____

    ● Slumpflation--_____

       _____

8. During periods of stagflation and slumpflation, economic policy-
    makers must decide whether to emphasize anti-inflationary
    measures and risk aggravating _____ or to
    emphasize expansionary measures and risk _____.

9. With the recurrence of stagflation in the early 1980s and the
    failure of income-expenditure policies to remedy that problem,
    Canada and the United States began to implement some supply-side
    measures to _____, _____,
    and _____.

VI. ECONOMIC COUNCILS

United States Council of Economic Advisers

1. The Employment Act of 1946 set up a Council of Economic Advisers
    (CEA) appointed by _____ with the
    advice and consent of _____.

2. Each of the _____ members must be exceptionally
    qualified to _____
       _____
       _____.

3. The Council reports to the President on _____

_____; the President in turn makes

recommendations for a program to promote _____

_____.

4. What is the function of the Council? _____

_____

_____

_____

5. The Employment Act also requires the President to transmit to
Congress an annual Economic Report which contains the following
three items:

   (1) _____

   (2) _____

   (3) _____

6. The Economic Report is referred to the Joint Economic Committee,

   which is composed of _____

   _____.

7. What are the three functions of the Joint Committee?

   (1) _____

   (2) _____

   (3) _____

   _____

8. What are the titles of two other persons who often make recommendations to the President and Congress on matters of economic policy?

   (1) _____

   (2) _____

Economic Council of Canada

9. The Economic Council of Canada is a(n) _____

   established in _____ that consists of _____

   _____

   _____.

10. The Economic Council is as representative as possible of the private sector across the country.

11. The Council's functions are to _____

    _____

    _____.

12. The Council reports to Parliament through _____

    and publishes an Annual Review in which it makes _____

    _____.

13. The responsibility of the Ministry of State for Economic

    Developed, created in _____, is to _____

    _____

    _____.

14. What is the title of another person who makes recommendations to the Prime Minister and Parliament on matters of economic policy?

    _____

SELECTED ANSWERS TO WORKING OUTLINE

II. POLICIES TO ALLEVIATE UNEMPLOYMENT

Methods of Increasing Government Spending

33. desired increase $\div$ MPS = level of government spending and
                                           taxation

   $20 billion $\div$ 1/2 = $40 billion

Direction of Emergency Government Spending

42. $\dfrac{\text{(desired employment level - current employment level)}}{\text{employment multiplier}}$ = number of new hires

   (58 million - 50 million) $\div$ 2 = 4 million.

TERMINOLOGY AND CONCEPTS INTRODUCED

fiscal drag--_____

_____

fiscal stimulus--_____

_____

tax remission plan--_____

_____

balanced budget multiplier effect--_____

_____

employment multiplier--_____

_____

Phillips curve--_____

_____

stagflation--_____

_____

slumpflation--_____

_____

SAMPLE OBJECTIVE QUESTIONS

1. The following statements can correctly be made about the fiscal policy of a national government that is attempting to bolster economic activity:

    A. Bank borrowing is usually recognized as the most feasible method of financing government spending to bring about an increase in the level of economic activity
    B. If the government could design a tax to absorb all "idle" funds that are not spent on consumption or investment, government spending would always be sufficient to bring total effective demand into equality with total output
    C. Printing new money to finance government spending eliminates the necessity of having the government go into debt to finance the increased spending
    D. If the government borrows funds through the sale of bonds to individuals who otherwise would use the funds for consumption or investment, government spending will have no net effect on the total effective demand

        (1) All of these
        (2) A, B and C only
        (3) A, B and D only
        (4) A, C and D only
        (5) B, C and D only

2. According to the advocates of income-expenditure analysis, the "balanced budget multiplier effect" occurs when a government operates with a balanced budget and

        (1) decreases government spending while holding taxes constant
        (2) taxes savings that otherwise would be spent and increases government spending
        (3) decreases both government spending and taxes
        (4) holds government spending constant while decreasing taxes

3. Based on historical statistics, a Phillips curve illustrates the theory that the lower the level of

        (1) the Gross National Product, the higher the level of prices
        (2) investment by firms, the higher the level of unemployment
        (3) the money supply, the higher the level of interest rates
        (4) unemployment, the higher the degree of inflation

4. When emergency government spending is used to raise the level of employment in economy, the government can either make direct monetary payments to the unemployed or allocated funds for public works and public service job programs. The following statements can correctly be made about these alternatives:

   A. Public works projects produce visible evidence of production efforts and expenditures
   B. Individuals spend direct monetary payments primarily for purchases of consumer goods
   C. Direct monetary payments tend to result in a greater increase in the multiplier effect than do public works projects
   D. Public works projects generate secondary and tertiary employment
   E. Public works projects can require the transportation and production of capital goods and supplies

        (1) All of these
        (2) A, B, D and E only
        (3) A, B and E only
        (4) A, C and E only
        (5) B, C and D only

ANALYSIS OF SAMPLE OBJECTIVE QUESTIONS

1. The correct choice is choice (1); all of the statements are correct.

2. Choice (2) is the correct answer. The balanced budget multiplier effect does not occur when a government decreases government spending (1 and 3) or decreases taxes (3 and 4) or holds taxes or spending constant (1 and 4), but only when the government increases taxes on idle funds and increases its spending proportionately.

3. The correct answer is choice (4). Choices (1), (2), and (3) are all incorrect. The Phillips curve depicts the relationship between un-employment and inflation.

4. The correct answer is choice (2); statements A, B, D, and E are all correct. Statement C is false. Direct monetary payments cause little if any increase in the multiplier effect, because direct payments are spent primarily for purchases of consumer goods and because direct payments do not entail the production of capital goods. Public works projects, on the other hand, require large amounts of capital goods and supplies which build up the multiplier effect and may even stimulate the accelerator effect.

REVIEW QUESTIONS

1. Discuss the effects of a hypothetical tax designed to absorb all those funds that are not spent on consumption or investment.

2. Summarize the methods by which government spending could be used as a means of raising effective demand.

3. Why is income-expenditure analysis commonly thought of only in terms of depression policies.

4. How can a rise in the MEC offset the anti-inflationary effects of a rise in the interest rate?

5. What are the merits of the methods by which the government can use surplus to combat inflation?

16
Business Cycles

OBJECTIVES

In this chapter, you will study the various stages of the business cycle and the effects of each of these stages on different elements of the economy. You will become familiar with indicators that analysts use to predict business cycles, and you will be introduced to some of the theories offered to explain the business cycle. Upon completion of this chapter, you should be able to

- Differentiate between minor cycles and major cycles

- Identify the adjustments that must be made before the intensity of a business cycle can be measured

- Describe the impact of one complete business cycle on each of the following forces within an economy: cost-price relationship, inventory level, liquidity preference, replacement demand, and psychological outlook

- Explain how exogenous forces can modify business cycles

- Distinguish among the three types of statistical indicators

WORKING OUTLINE

I. **ACTUAL VERSUS POTENTIAL OUTPUT**

   1. One of the striking features of an industrial economy is its

      dynamism, which is to say that an industrial economy does not

      _____.

2. The importance of maximizing income and output is best realized

when the losses from _____ or even _____

are considered.

 ● Even in the relative prosperity of the past few decades, much

   has been lost in the way of production and employment through

   _____ or _____

   and the failure of the economy to maintain _____

   _____.

II. THE BUSINESS CYCLE

1. National income is subject to various types of disturbance, but

   the most pronounced of these is the business cycle, which is a

   process of _____ over a time span longer

   than _____.

2. All parts of the economy display marked changes in activity as

   they move through the phases of _____

   _____.

3. Cyclical fluctuations are found in economies throughout the

   world, but they appear most clearly in those economies where

   _____ and _____ prevail.

Types and Length of Cycles

4. An analysis of historical data reveals that business fluctuations
   may be classified as minor cycles or major cycles. Define each
   of these terms.

● Minor cycles--_____

_____

● Major cycles--_____

_____

5. Minor cycles generally occur every _____.

6. Although business cycle data indicate that major cycles occur

about _____, neither the United

States nor Canada has experienced a major cycle since _____.

● This may be due to the use of modern _____ and

_____ measures and the built-in economic stimulus of

_____.

7. List three other types of cycles or fluctuations.

(1) _____ (3) _____

(2) _____

Phases and Measurement of the Cycle

8. What circumstances characterize each of the following phases of
the business cycle?

● Prosperity--_____

● Recession--_____

● Depression--_____

● Recovery--_____

9. A business cycle consists of a series of changes that includes

_____.

10. Customarily, a mild depression is referred to as _____

_____ .

11. What definition did the National Bureau of Economic Research

(NBER) give to <u>recession</u>? _____

_____

 • If this definition is considered correct, then there is some
 confusion regarding the meaning of <u>depression</u>.

12. What characteristics have led analysts to consider the double-dip

recession of 1980 and 1982 as a depression? _____

_____

_____

13. Although we have more or less definite measurements of the length

of the _____ and even the length of the _____

_____ , it

is difficult to obtain a conclusive measurement of the average

length of _____ .

14. It is possible to measure the degree of business fluctuation, as

long as allowances are made for _____

_____ other than those that are

inherent in the business cycle.

15. Name and define the four forces or types of economic change that
affect the level of business activity at any time.

(1) _____

_____

(2) _____

_____

(3) _____

_____

(4) _____

_____

16. How can the intensity of the business cycle be determined?

_____

_____

Pattern of the Cycle

17. Once a downturn has started, there is a(n) _____

_____ that tends to augment

the downswing.

18. During the downswing, forces eventually come into play to

_____ and to _____.

19. Once the upward motion begins, _____

_____ are such that the upswing is augmented.

20. During prosperity, however, forces build up that eventually

_____.

21. Endogenous forces and exogenous forces operate to bring about
business cycles. Define these terms and give six examples of
each.

● Endogenous forces-- _____

_____

(1) _____ (4) _____

(2) _____ (5) _____

(3) _____ (6) _____

● Exogenous forces-- _____

_____

(1) _____ (4) _____

(2) _____ (5) _____

(3) _____ (6) _____

III. DEPRESSION

Cost-Price Relationship

1. During a depression, _____, _____, and _____

   are at a comparatively low ebb.

2. Low income leads to a low demand for _____;

   low demand in a period of ample supply generally _____

   _____ or _____.

3. State the reason that each of the following elements would be at
   a low level during a depression:

   ● Cost--_____

   _____

   ● Profits--_____

   _____

   ● Investment--_____

   _____

Inventory Adjustment and Borrowing

4. In the early phases of a depression, inventories may be rather high because of _____.

5. What causes inventories to dwindle? _____
    _____

6. Since production is at a low level, businesses have little need for _____.

7. Business loans fall off substantially during a depression.

    ● Many businesses are reluctant to borrow because _____ _____.

    ● Many firms that would like to borrow for refinancing are _____ and cannot obtain loans.

8. The relatively high level of excess reserves and the low demand for loans will generally force _____.

Liquidity Preference and Saving

9. Why is there a strong liquidity preference during a depression?

    _____

    _____

10. As incomes are lowered, the propensity to consume _____, while the propensity to save _____.

11. However, although individuals are spending a larger percentage of income, the total amount of spending on consumption is _____ than it was during the previous prosperity period.

Replacement Demand

12. When production is at less than full capacity, businesses have less need to _____.

13. Consumers tend to _____ their durable goods instead of _____.

Psychological Forces

14. During a depression, with _____, _____, _____, _____, and _____ low, a pessimistic attitude prevails.

15. Under such conditions, businesses are reluctant to _____, and consumers are more cautious in _____ and cut down on _____.

16. The actions of businesses and individuals during a depression have a tendency to hold down the _____ and make the _____ more difficult.

IV. RECOVERY

Starters

1. Often _____, such as population increase, innovation, war, or the use of monetary or fiscal policy cause the end of a depression.

2. Even without such factors, however, the relationships among certain of the basic elements of the business cycle may eventually _____ and initiate an upward movement in the economy.

3. After a depression has existed for a period, a better _____ relationship develops.

4. Costs generally lag behind prices in their movements during the cycle.

   ● On a downturn, _____ fall first and at a more rapid rate than _____.

   ● Prices reach their low point while costs are _____.

   ● Eventually costs dip lower than prices, so that it again becomes _____ for businesses to produce certain goods.

   ● Prices frequently begin to rise _____ and _____ than costs.

   ● On the upward swing of the cycle, the margin between price and cost is widened, resulting in _____ and

   _____.

5. Competition is a major factor in reducing costs below prices.

6. The method of handling inventories can spur production.

   ● For the first several months of a depression, _____ is filled out of inventories.

   ● Eventually inventories become depleted, and they have to be

   _____.

- When inventories stabilize at lower levels, most current sales have to be _____ _____.

7. The accumulation of _____ and the downward pressure on _____ may encourage some borrowing by business.

8. Although firms and individuals have a tendency to postpone replacement of _____ and _____ during a depression, they cannot do so forever.

   - Eventually such goods will wear out.

   - Firms may replace old machinery with improved machinery that can increase _____.

9. The pessimistic outlook of businesses and individuals during a depression is subject to change.

   - Businesses and individuals increase consumption and investment in anticipation of _____.

10. In summary, a favorable change in any of the following five areas may lead to an increase in production:

    (1) _____   (4) _____

    (2) _____   (5 _____

    (3) _____

11. Sometimes the increase in production is insufficient to _____ _____.

289

Production, Employment, and Income

12. The force that leads an economy out of depression is the _____

_____.

13. If production increases, _____ and _____ will

naturally increase.

14. With higher _____, people increase their _____.

15. Prices remain fairly constant during the early part of the

recovery since _____

_____. When demand

increases sufficiently, prices begin _____.

16. Cost remains relatively low during the early part of the recovery

since _____

_____.

17. Profits increase as _____.

18. Larger inventories are held in the expectation of _____.

19. Increased profits bring about increased _____, which in

turn leads to greater demand for _____.

   ● Theoretically, excess reserves should then decrease, but

   higher _____ often forestall the decrease of

   excess reserves until late in the _____

   or well into the _____.

   ● As a result, _____ rise slowly.

20. As incomes increase, there is a weakening of _____

    _____.

V.   PROSPERITY

1. List three ill effects that may develop during prosperity.

    (1) _____   (3) _____

    (2) _____

Cost-Price Relationship

2. As _____, _____, and _____ begin to

    rise, the interactions of the endogenous forces are such that

    they augment the upswing.

3. With increased production, the economy reaches the "bottleneck"

    stage, a period in which _____

    and _____.

    This causes an upward price movement.

4. Since prices increase faster than do _____, high

    profits occur.

5. High profits and greater sales lead to large _____,

    which emphasize the incentives for _____.

Inventory Adjustment

6. The quantity of inventory a merchant or producer keeps on hand

    usually is related to _____.

    ● When sales increase, the size of inventories _____.

291

● Therefore, production must increase not only to _____ _____ but also to _____.

7. A second force, the price factor, also accelerates inventory accumulation. Explain how this occurs. _____

_____

Replacement Demand

8. There is a tendency during a period of prosperity to replace worn out assets at _____ and to add new assets to meet the _____.

9. This replacement becomes all the more feasible when _____ _____.

Liquidity Preference and Saving

10. Early during prosperity, prices are low, but eventually they begin to rise.

● As prices begin to rise, _____ decreases because the value of money begins to _____.

11. An increase in the MPS appears, but it is usually not sufficient to _____.

12. If the level of economic activity reaches the stage of full employment, further increases in _____, _____, _____, and such can lead only to _____.

292

VI. RECESSION

Cost-Price Relationship

1. While production, employment, and income are at their peak, some

   _____ may appear.

   • Sometimes the mere fact that demand begins to _____

   _____, instead of continuing to _____

   _____, can cause difficulty.

2. The MPC declines as incomes _____.

3. The price level eventually stabilizes, but costs continue to increase because of competition for relatively scarce factors of production.

   • The rising costs gradually eliminate some of the _____,

   which tends to make businesses more cautious about _____.

Inventory Adjustment

4. When demand _____ and prices _____ or

   _____, wholesalers will attempt to deplete excess

   inventory by meeting current demand _____,

   rather than ordering from the producer.

5. If the price level is dropping, the wholesaler not only reduces

   excess stock, but reduces the _____.

6. According to some economists, _____

   _____ play a major role in the cause of

   business cycles.

Replacement Demand

7. Because recession brings about a reduction in demand, businesses find it unnecessary to replace _____.

8. Consumers begin postponing the purchase of _____.

    ● The eventual fall of prices causes further postponement of purchases as consumers _____

    _____.

Liquidity Preference and Savings

9. Falling prices strengthen the _____ as the value of money _____.

10. The propensity to save _____ with the decrease in incomes.

    ● Individuals and families may desire to save even more than previously, but they may be unable to do so because of _____ _____ or _____.

Psychological Outlook

11. As the recession gets under way, the changing relationships of the endogenous elements are such that they tend to _____

    _____.

12. The recession continues to deepen until somewhere along the way the stage of depression is reached, completing the business cycle.

VII. FACTORS THAT MAY MODIFY THE BUSINESS CYCLE

1. The duration and the intensity of fluctuations in the economy

   can be modified by the use of _____, _____, and

   _____ measures.

2. Because the pattern of fluctuations is so well-established,

   action can be taken to avoid the two extremes of the cycle--

   _____ and _____.

3. External forces affect the level of economic activity and often
   generate business fluctuations. List four examples of external
   forces which can have such an impact.

   (1) _____ (3) _____

   (2) _____ (4) _____

4. The typical pattern of the business cycle is modified to the
   extent that competition in the economy is imperfect. Cite three
   examples.

   (1) _____

   (2) _____

   (3) _____

5. In any particular cycle, one or more of the endogenous elements
   may act contrary to its usual movement, yet, the overall pattern
   will still be more or less the same.

VIII. BUSINESS CYCLE INDICATORS

1. For purposes of analyzing business cycles, statistical indicators
   are usually divided into the following three types:

   (1) _____ (3) _____

   (2) _____

Representative Indicators

2. Although representative indicators are usually indexes that

   measure _____,

   those that measure _____

   will reflect to some degree what is happening to the economy as a

   whole.

3. Cite four examples of reliable representative indicators.

   (1) _____ (3) _____

   (2) _____ (4) _____

Composite Indicators

4. Composite indicators give a good indication of the general level

   of business activity because they usually measure

   _____

   _____.

5. List four examples of widely used composite indicators.

   (1) _____ (3) _____

   (2) _____ (4) _____

General Business Indicators

6. Most general business indicators combine _____

   _____.

7. The Business Week Index reflects the combined movement of several
   individual series in the United States.

8. Identify and describe the three types of statistical indicators of business-cycle changes published by the Statistical Indicator Associates.

   (1) _____

   _____

   (2) _____

   _____

   (3) _____

   _____

9. The _Trendicator_, published by the Royal Bank, tracks _____

   _____ for the Canadian economy.

10. List four other sources of indicators and other current data about the Canadian economy.

    (1) _____

    (2) _____

    (3) _____

    (4) _____

11. By following the business cycle indicators closely, business

    cycle analysts may be able to anticipate pending changes in the

    level of business activity and make proper adjustments in

    _____, _____, _____, and

    _____ to compensate for expected changes in

    business activity.

IX. CAUSES OF THE BUSINESS CYCLE

1. Numerous theories have been offered to explain business fluctuations. Although no one theory completely explains the cause of

business cycles, a study of the various theories permits a better understanding of the possible causes of cycles.

2. Sometimes the theories are similar, and the differences are only a matter of emphasis.

3. The business cycle theories can be classified in the following four major categories:

(1) _____   (3) _____

(2) _____   (4) _____

Real or Physical Causes

4. According to the innovation theory, business cycles are caused by

innovations in the form of _____, _____,

_____, or _____, which

lead to increased _____, _____ and

_____ in the economy.

● If the firms which introduce the innovations are successful,

others will imitate them until a point of _____

is eventually reached.

● The reaction to this situation brings about a(n) _____

in the form of _____ production, employ-

ment, and income.

● Economic analysts who hold to this theory contend that the

decline will be _____ than the

expansion, and thus there will be _____

in the economy as a result of innovation.

5. The intensity and duration of the cycle brought about by such an

innovation depend on _____.

6. What are the agricultural theories of the business cycle? _____

_____

_____

7. According to the accelerator theory, an increase in the demand

for _____ may lead to a greater than pro-

portional increase in the demand for _____. As

consumers demand _____, the firm will not

require additional machines, so the demand for machines will

decrease in greater proportion than the _____

_____.

Psychological Causes

8. The psychological theory is the foundation for the theory of

rational expectations; therefore, the psychological theory has

has already been introduced. To summarize, the psychological

theory holds that when investors and consumers react according to

some belief about future conditions, _____

_____.

9. According to the psychological theory, what roles are played
   by the following elements?

   • The actions of business leaders--_____

   _____

   • Competition--_____

   _____

299

Monetary Causes

10. Most monetary theories are based on the premise that _____

    _____

    _____ .

11. Monetary theorists maintain that to eliminate the business cycle

    it is necessary to _____ .

    ● How do banks defend their role? _____

      _____

      _____

Spending and Saving Causes

12. The two broad categories of spending and saving theories are

    (1) _____ (2) _____

13. The major underconsumption theory holds that the economy

    distributes enough purchasing power to _____

    _____ , but that not all the

    income or purchasing power is _____ .

    ● Therefore, _____ will be reduced, causing

      a decrease in _____ and _____ .

14. Some less popular underconsumption theories hold that the economy

    does not distribute enough _____ among the

    _____ to permit the purchase of _____

    _____ .

15. Some of the leading underconsumption theorists maintain that the

    basic cause of business cycles is the _____

    _____.

16. List five measures that underconsumption theorists believe can
    lessen that inequality.

    (1) _____

    (2) _____

    (3) _____

    (4) _____

    (5) _____

17. The underinvestment theory holds that:

    ● Income in the economy is _____.

    ● To clear all goods off the market, _____

      _____ must take place.

    ● Spending on consumption is less than _____.

    ● Therefore, the difference must be made up in the form of

      _____

      _____.

18. According to underinvestment theorists, the relationship between
    the amount of investment spending and the size of the gap between
    income and consumer spending affects the economy. Three such
    relationships are listed in the left-hand column below. In the
    blank beside each relationship, write the letter identifying the

state of the economy given in the right-hand column that would correspond to that relationship.

_____(1)Investment spending > gap   a.   Economy experiences a
between income and   downswing
consumer spending

_____(2)Investment spending = gap   b.   Economy experiences an
between consumer income   upswing
and consumer spending

_____(3)Investment spending < gap   c.   Economy is in
between income and   equilibrium
consumer spending

19. The underinvestment theory summarized here is the crux of

_____.

TERMINOLOGY AND CONCEPTS INTRODUCED

business cycle--_____

_____

minor cycles--_____

_____

major cycles--_____

_____

prosperity--_____

_____

recession--_____

_____

depression--_____

_____

302

recovery--_____

_____

trend--_____

_____

seasonal variations--_____

_____

irregular (random) fluctuations--_____

_____

cyclical fluctuations--_____

_____

endogenous forces--_____

_____

exogenous forces--_____

_____

representative indicators--_____

_____

composite indicators--_____

_____

general business indicators--_____

_____

leading indicators--_____

_____

roughly coincident indicators--_____

_____

lagging indicators--_____

_____

innovation theory--_____

_____

agricultural theories--_____

_____

accelerator theory--_____

_____

psychological theory--_____

_____

theory of rational expectations--_____

_____

monetary theories--_____

_____

underconsumption theories--_____

_____

underinvestment theories--_____

_____

SAMPLE OBJECTIVE QUESTIONS

1. The level of business activity at any time is affected by various types of economic change. The average growth or decline in the economy over an extended period is referred to by economists as a

    (1) trend
    (2) cyclical fluctuation
    (3) random fluctuation
    (4) seasonal variation

2. The elements operating to bring about business cycles are categorized as being either endogenous (internal) forces or exogenous (external) forces. The following forces usually are considered to be endogenous to the business cycle:

    A. Inventories
    B. Population growth
    C. Credit
    D. Demand

        (1) All of these
        (2) A, B and C only
        (3) A, C and D only
        (4) B and D only
        (5) C and D only

3. Among the changes that may occur during a depression which help to start the economy on the road to recovery are the following:

    A. Costs of production dip to a point below prices such that production becomes more profitable
    B. The value of money rises, causing the liquidity preference of individuals to become stronger
    C. Business inventories become so depleted that replacement becomes necessary
    D. Interest rates reach a low point which encourages borrowing by business
    E. Capital goods and machinery wear out and must be replaced

        (1) All of these
        (2) A, B, C and E only
        (3) A, C, D and E only
        (4) A, C and D only
        (5) B, D and E only

4. Business cycle indicators reflect changes in business activity. The gross national product (GNP) is an example of a business indicator known as a

        (1) representative indicator
        (2) leading indicator
        (3) lagging indicator
        (4) composite indicator

5. One business cycle theory proposes that business cycles can be eliminated or modified by the use of steeply progressive income taxes, federally sponsored income maintenance programs, and monopolistic pricing regulations. This business cycle theory is known as the

    (1) monetary theory
    (2) innovation theory
    (3) underinvestment theory
    (4) underconsumption theory

ANALYSIS OF SAMPLE OBJECTIVE QUESTIONS

1. The correct answer is choice (1). Seasonal variations (4) are recurring fluctuations in business activity. Cyclical fluctuations (2) are the changes in the level of business activity that are known as business cycles. Random fluctuations (3) in business activity are caused by some unexpected or unusual event. None of these three kinds of economic change exhibits the sustained directional movement of the trend as it charts the average change in the economy over a period such as 30 to 50 years.

2. Choice (3) is the correct answer; statements A, C, and D are all correct. Statement B is incorrect, because population is an example of an exogenous force.

3. The correct answer is choice (3); statements A, C, D, and E are all true. Statement B is an incorrect statement. During a recession, the value of money rises causing the liquidity preference of individuals to become stronger; this means that individuals try to convert their idle assets into money. However, instead of starting the economy on the road to recovery, this tendency augments the downward movement in the economy. If the liquidity preference were to decrease, so that individuals converted their money assets into property and other real goods, this might initiate an upward movement in the economy.

4. Choice (4) is the correct answer. Representative indicators (1) only attempt to measure changes in a segment of business activity. Leading indicators (2) precede general business activity, and lagging indicators (3) follow general business activity. The GNP is a widely used example of a composite indicator.

5. The correct answer is choice (4); choices (1), (2), and (3) are all incorrect. The underconsumption theorists maintain that the primary cause of the business cycle is the unequal distribution of income in modern society. The measures listed in this question are all means of lessening that inequality.

REVIEW QUESTIONS

1. Why is it difficult to obtain a conclusive measurement of the average length of each of the four phases of the business cycle?

2. Explain fully how an external force such as war can affect the level of economic activity and generate business fluctuations.

3. Some economists and government officials in the early 1960s suggested that the theory of business cycles was obsolete. What led them to this belief? Have the events since that time confirmed their conclusion?

4. The agricultural theories of the business cycle were very popular early in this century. To what extent are these theories valid today?

17

Taxation, Budgetary Policy, and the National Debt

OBJECTIVES

In this chapter, you will study the principles of taxation--how taxes are determined, who bears the burden of taxes, and the purposes behind taxation. You will see how the governments of Canada and the United States have tried to use budgetary policy and the national debt to stabilize economic activity. You will become acquainted with the issues raised by the presence of large national debts in the United States and Canada. Upon completion of this chapter, you should be able to

- List the desirable characteristics of a tax

- Discuss the three theories of fair apportionment of the tax burden

- Distinguish among the four tax-rate structures

- Explain the concept of shifting the tax burden

- Describe the principal objectives of taxation

- Identify the effects associated with a large national debt

- Summarize the arguments for and against a statutory ceiling on national debt

WORKING OUTLINE

Introduction

1. Taxation is the institutional arrangement for _____

_____.

2. List two examples of services that are associated with each of the following levels of government:

● Federal government--

(1) _____ (2) _____

● State/provincial and local governments--

(1) _____ (2) _____

3. Today all three levels of government participate in providing

some services, such as _____ and _____

_____.

I.   TAXATION

1. List two sources of taxes that have traditionally been associated with each of the following levels of government:

● Federal government--

(1) _____ (2) _____

● State/provincial and local governments--

(1) _____ (2) _____

Characteristics of a Tax

2. List five criteria that a government usually weighs in considering whether to implement a tax:

(1) _____

(2) _____

(3) _____

_____

(4) _____

(5) _____

_____

Equity or Fairness in Taxation

3. Three proposals for apportioning the tax burden fairly are

    (1) _____

    (2) _____

    (3) _____

4. The cost-of-service theory suggests that individuals should con-

    tribute to the cost of government in proportion to

    _____

    _____.

5. State two reasons why the cost-of-service theory is inappropriate
    for all but a few minor government services.

    (1) _____

    (2) _____

6. The benefit-received theory of taxation holds that individuals

    should contribute to the cost of government in proportion to

    _____

    _____.

7. The benefit-received theory is closely related to _____

    _____.

8. On what premise are real estate taxes based?

    _____

    _____

    _____

9. Although the benefit-received theory is not practicable as a guide for the formulation of taxes in general, the theory is followed, to a certain extent, in cases such as _____ taxes and _____ fees.

10. The most commonly accepted theory of taxation is that taxes should be based on _____.

11. One popular idea is that taxes should be assessed _____ _____ in accordance with some standard such as property value or income.

12. The equality-of-sacrifice doctrine of taxation is based upon the law of diminishing marginal utility of income, which states

_____

_____

_____.

13. A majority of persons most likely agree that a proportional tax is much more of a hardship on a low-income family (one that is already living close to the _____) than on a family with a larger income.

14. Some individuals contend that a proportional tax calls for equal sacrifice from upper- and lower-income families. Explain the thinking behind this argument. _____

_____

_____

II. THE TAX-RATE STRUCTURE

1. The tax-rate structure determines the amounts that _____

   _____ .

2. The amount of a tax is determined by applying the tax rate to the
   tax base. Define the following terms:

   ● Tax rate-- _____

   ● Tax base-- _____

3. The relationship of a given tax rate to the size of the tax base
   can be described by one of the following four terms:

   (1) _____   (3) _____

   (2) _____   (4) _____

Proportional Rates

4. What is a proportional tax rate? _____

   _____

5. Cite two arguments in favor of a proportional tax rate.

   (1) _____

   (2) _____

6. The application of a proportional tax-rate structure may not

   result in imposing _____ upon tax-

   payers.

Progressive Rates

7. Because most people believe that _____

   should be used as a criterion for taxation, some taxes are

   applied at a progressive rate.

8. A progressive tax rate is one in which _____

_____ .

   ● An example of a progressive tax rate is a tax of 1 percent on

     the first $1,000 of taxable income, 2 percent on the second

     $1,000, and so on. What happens to all income beyond

     $100,000 if this rate of progression is continued? _____

     _____

9. Opponents argue that progressive taxes are unfair because

_____

_____ .

10. In North America, there is a tendency to sanction _____

_____ .

11. One argument put forth by opponents of progressive taxes has to

    do with the poor. Explain this argument. _____

_____

_____

_____

Degressive Rates

12. A degressive tax rate calls for the payment of _____

_____

_____, but the payments are not _____

_____. A degressive tax is a progressive tax

for which the rate _____ at a decreasing rate.

13. Degressive taxes avoid one drawback of progressive taxes, which is that once a progressive rate structure is adopted, the logical stopping place tends to approach 100 percent, which results in _____ of the value of the tax base from that point on.

14. In practice, income taxes are usually _____ up to a certain level of income, then _____ for an additional level of income, after which they remain _____
_____.

Regressive Rates

15. A regressive tax rate is one that _____
_____.

16. Why do opponents of a sales tax claim that it is a regressive tax? _____
_____
_____

    Is this claim accurate? _____ Why or why not? _____
_____
_____

17. Some taxes have elements of one or more different rates in their structure.

18. Types of taxes are listed in the left-hand column below. In the blank beside each type of tax, write the letter identifying the description in the right-hand column that best matches that tax.

____(1)Degressive tax   a. The rate decreases as the base increases

____(2)Progressive tax   b. The rate increase keeps pace with the rate of increase in the base

____(3)Proportional tax   c. The rate increases as the base increases, but the rate increases at a decreasing rate

____(4)Regressive tax   d. The rate remains the same while the base increases

III. THE TAX BURDEN

1. The burden of a tax does not always rest on the person or the firm paying the tax. Instead, shifting taxes is the process of

_____

_____.

2. Give an example of shifting taxes. _____

_____

_____

3. Although many taxes can be shifted, it is not possible to shift the burden of some taxes, such as a tax on _____.

4. The impact of a tax is the _____

_____.

5. What is the incidence of a tax? _____

_____

6. Define and give two examples of the <u>effect of a tax.</u> _____

   _____

   (1) _____

   (2) _____

7. Define the following two terms:

   ● Direct tax--_____

   ● Indirect tax--_____

IV. PURPOSES OF TAXATION

Cover the Costs of Government

1. For decades the primary purpose of taxation was to _____

   _____

   _____

2. During these times, a balanced budget was a perennial objective.

   ● What three actions could government take to assure that it
     would achieve this objective if prosperity abounded and tax
     revenues were pointing toward a surplus?

     (1) _____

     (2) _____

     (3) _____

   ● What was the government expected to do in order to meet its

     objective during a period of economic slack when falling tax

     revenues threatened a deficit? _____

     _____

316

Redistribute Income and Wealth

3. How have the governments of Canada and the United States used

   taxation as a means of redistributing income and wealth? _____

   _____

   _____

   _____

4. Relying on the ability-to-pay concept, income tax revenues in the
   general fund are used to provide services such as the following:

   (1) _____

   (2) _____

   (3) _____

Stabilize Economic Activity

5. Over the past forty years, Canada and the United States have
   established a policy of using taxation and government spending
   for the purpose of stabilizing economic activity.

   ● Both countries have developed a set of fiscal measures to

   _____ and to _____

   _____.

   ● The use of these fiscal measures involves the federal budget

   and has an effect on _____ and on _____.

Types of Budgets

6. Types of national budgets are listed in the left-hand column
   below. In the blank beside each type of budget, write the letter
   identifying the relationship between government spending and

revenue from taxes given in the right-hand column that
accompanies that type of budget.

    ___(1)Balanced budget a. Government spending > revenue from
                                          taxes

    ___(2)Deficit budget   b. Government spending = revenue from
                                          taxes

    ___(3)Surplus budget c. Government spending < revenue from
                                          taxes

7. A balanced budget generally has a(n) _____ effect on

the economy because total spending in the economy _____

_____.

8. How is it possible that a balanced budget can bring about an

expansionary effect in the economy? _____

_____

9. A deficit budget will generally increase the level of economic

activity or will be inflationary, depending on the _____

_____.

  ● If the government _____

_____, the total effective demand of

the economy will be increased.

  ● Therefore, the level of economic activity will increase if

_____, and

inflation will occur if _____

_____.

10. For this reason, a deficit budget is frequently referred to as

    _____ .

11. The effects of the deficit budget will be offset to some extent

    if the government _____

    _____ .

12. A surplus budget results in a(n) _____ in effective

    demand.

13. A surplus budget is often considered by some as a fiscal drag on
    the economy.

    ● This drag effect would be modified to the extent that

      _____

      _____ .

    ● This drag effect would be offset if the government were to

      _____ .

14. At times, a surplus budget may be used as an anti-inflationary

    measure to _____ .

V. PROBLEMS OF THE NATIONAL DEBT

1. The national debt can be affected by the _____ ,

   _____ , and _____ of the federal

   budget.

2. The governments of Canada and the United States have had limited
   experience with budgetary policy as a means of stabilizing
   business activity.

- It is difficult, therefore, to determine whether either country

  can _____ deficits and surpluses accurately

  and have them of proper _____ to act as

  stabilizers of the economy.

- Furthermore, neither country has had sufficient experience to

  determine whether, in the absence of _____,

  the deficits and surpluses can offset each other sufficiently

  to _____.

Bankruptcy

3. In both Canada and the United States, many people think that the

   national debt could become so large that it would bankrupt their

   nation. This misunderstanding arises from the failure to

   distinguish clearly the _____ of government

   financing and the power of the federal government to _____

   _____.

4. When a government borrows and repays funds, this type of

   financing is more like the financial transactions taking place

   within _____ than the type of financing practiced

   by _____.

- Whenever a business does not have sufficient cash or current

  assets to pay off its current debts, it lacks _____.

  Since the money used to pay business debt actually leaves the

  firm, the business is unable to repay its debt.

● When one member of a family borrows money from another family member, there is no _____ of assets nor is there any money leaving the family.

5. When a federal government borrows money, it borrows primarily from _____, _____, and _____ within the economy.

6. When a federal government makes repayment on its debt, the money stays _____, so there is no _____ in total assets.

7. The government's ability to repay is governed only by the total _____ of the economy or, more immediately, by the total _____ of the economy and the government's ability to _____.

8. Theoretically, as long as national income is larger than the national debt, the government could tax a sufficient amount to _____, though in practice such an action would not be taken.

9. The taxation and repayment of the debt would merely cause a(n) _____ inside the economy. The total income or assets of the economy would be the same after _____ as before.

10. Some allowance would have to be made for the fact that, for both

    Canada and the United States, foreigners hold _____

    _____ .

11. Over a long period, the governments of Canada and the United

    States could operate at surpluses sufficient to _____

    _____ . Surpluses obtained during _____

    could be used to pay the debt during periods of _____

    in the economy.

Effect of Redistribution of Income

12. List two reasons why governments are reluctant to reduce the debt
    by sizable amounts.

    (1) _____

    (2) _____

13. If the debt were to be paid off on a large-scale basis, heavy

    taxes would reduce _____ , especially

    among _____ .

14. Whether such a reduction in _____ would be

    offset when the government used tax money to pay off the debt

    would depend on what the recipients of debt repayments would

    _____ .

15. The total propensity to _____ or to _____ could

    be less for debt holders who receive repayment than for taxpayers

    in total.

322

16. Lower income groups do not hold much of the federal debt; instead, it is held primarily by _____, _____, _____, and _____ _____.

17. If the debt were repaid during _____, and if the debt holders would _____ _____ at the time the debts were re- paid, repaying the debt would not have an adverse effect on the economy.

18. It would be best, however, to pay off the debt during periods of _____ with money obtained through taxation during a(n) _____ or _____ period.

Burden of the Debt

19. It is often thought that when the debt is not paid during _____ _____, the burden of paying the debt is passed on to future generations.

20. If we are considering the total economy, it is impossible to _____.

21. The real cost of the debt to the total economy can only be measured by the cost of _____ _____.

22. The people in the economy at the time the debt was incurred shouldered the real burden of the debt through the _____ in consumer production.

23. For the economy as a whole, debt repayment, whether repaid _____ or _____, will not cost anything in terms of goods and services.

24. As a result of the _____ that takes place at the time the debt is repaid, some individuals and firms may suffer a loss of purchasing power; but this will be offset by gains to other individuals and firms, and no _____ _____ in purchasing power in the economy will take place.

25. Although the cost of the debt cannot be passed on to future generations from the viewpoint of the total economy, the burden for _____ can be passed on to future generations.

26. The particular individuals taxed to pay the debt have to give up _____, and therefore they are burdened to the extent that they are taxed.

27. If the government, instead of paying off the debt in a relatively short period, were to postpone payment for a genera-tion or two, the burden of the debt would have been passed to individuals of future generations.

28. One reason the government is reluctant to pay off the national debt is the effect of repayment on the _____.

29. When an individual or a business loans money to the government, there is no _____ in the money supply; however, if a bank loans money to the government and pays for the bonds through the creation of _____, the money supply is increased.

30. What does the government do when it monetizes the debt? _____

    _____

    _____

31. When the government goes into debt by borrowing from the banks, it adds _____ pressures to the economy.

32. A decrease in the money supply will have a tendency to decrease the _____ and/or decrease the _____, unless offset by some other force.

33. The money supply will be decreased when the debt is _____.

34. What does the government do when it demonetizes the debt? _____

    _____

    _____

35. If the government were to reduce the federal debt by sizable amounts over a relatively short period, the money supply might be _____ to such an extent that it would have an adverse effect on the _____.

36. Under what circumstances could payment of the debt be beneficial to the economy by reducing inflationary pressures? _____

_____

_____

Size of the Debt

37. In both Canada and the United States, the national debt has not been reduced absolutely, but the size of the debt relative to _____ has been reduced because of increased _____ and higher _____.

38. Decreasing income, resulting from either a falling _____ or a drop in production or employment would increase the _____ relative to income and make _____ more burdensome.

Refunding the Debt

39. Since government debt obligations usually reach maturity at a time when the federal treasury does not have the money to pay them, the federal government generally will _____ _____ to raise money to pay off the matured obligations.

   • This refunding may be difficult to accomplish.

   • The government may be forced to pay _____ _____ when it borrows funds for this purpose.

Burden of Interest Payments

40. Federal taxation for the payment of interest on the national debt does not impose _____ on the economy as a whole, but it does cause _____ and, therefore, a burden to individuals and firms in the economy.

41. If the government had originally _____ _____, or if the government had _____, it would have imposed a smaller total burden on the individuals than it does when the debt repayment is postponed.

42. With the postponement of the debt, the redistribution of income necessary to retire the debt is not only the amount of _____, but also the _____.

43. What happens when the interest rate rises? _____ _____

44. What two hardships do individuals and firms have to choose between regarding the timing of the repayment of national debt?

    (1) _____

    (2) _____

Productivity of the Debt

45. The money that a business borrows can increase its _____ and enhance its _____.

46. Individuals borrow to enhance their _____ ,and

to give them greater _____ of current consumption.

47. Government debt can also increase consumers' satisfaction by

financing projects such as the _____

_____ and the _____ .

48. A government must decide whether increased _____

and the utility of _____ are of greater

value than the disutility of _____ .

VI. DEBT CEILING

1. The United States has a statutory limit or ceiling on its
   national debt.

2. A federal deficit accompanied by a rise in the debt ceiling will

   generally provoke more opposition than a deficit that _____

   _____ .

3. How does the cause of debt affect Congressional acceptance of

   debt ceiling increases? _____

   _____

4. State three arguments against the debt ceiling.

   (1) _____

   _____

   (2) _____

   _____

   (3) _____

   _____

5. Proponents of the debt ceiling stress that it is needed to

   _____ government spending and that it prevents

   _____.

6. Insofar as the ceiling limits deficits in the annual budget, it

   makes the taxpayers more conscious of the _____

   _____.

7. Although Canada has no statutory ceiling on its national debt, or

   the interest rate it can pay, the Minister of Finance must

   _____ in order to borrow funds.

TERMINOLOGY AND CONCEPTS INTRODUCED

cost-of-service theory--_____

_____

benefit-received theory--_____

_____

ability-to-pay theory--_____

_____

proportional standard--_____

_____

equality-of-sacrifice doctrine--_____

_____

tax rate--_____

_____

tax base--_____

_____

proportional tax rate--_____

_____

progressive tax rate--_____

_____

degressive tax rate--_____

_____

regressive tax rate--_____

_____

shifting taxes--_____

_____

impact of a tax--_____

_____

incidence of a tax--_____

_____

effect of a tax--_____

_____

direct tax--_____

_____

indirected tax--_____

_____

balanced budget--_____

_____

deficit budget-- _____

_____

surplus budget-- _____

_____

monetizing the debt-- _____

_____

demonetizing the debt-- _____

_____

SAMPLE OBJECTIVE QUESTIONS

1. The relationship of tax rates to changes in the tax base is indicated
    by the terms proportional, progressive, degressive, and regressive.
    The following statements can correctly be made about these categories
    of tax rate structures:

    A. According to a proportional tax rate structure, the tax rate
        remains the same regardless of the size of the tax base
    B. A degressive tax rate calls for the payment of a larger amount
        of tax as the size of the base increases, but the payments are
        not progressively larger
    C. A tax rate structure according to which the first $1,000 of
        taxable income is taxed at 1 percent, the second $1,000 of
        income is taxed at 2 percent, and so on, is said to be
        progressive
    D. According to a regressive tax rate structure, the tax rate
        decreases as the size of the tax base decreases

        (1) All of these
        (2) A, B and C only
        (3) A, B and D only
        (4) B, C and D only
        (5) A and C only

2. The type of budget a nation has will affect that nation's level of
    economic activity to some degree. For example, a deficit budget can

        (1) increase the total effective demand of the economy
        (2) decrease the level of economic activity
        (3) have a neutral effect on the economy
        (4) serve as a fiscal drag on the economy

331

3. The following statements can correctly be made about a large national debt:

   A. Attempts to pay off the debt through taxation would reduce the total income of the nation
   B. Repayment of the debt could create a redistribution of income that would decrease effective demand
   C. In terms of the total economy, the real cost of the national debt is passed on to future generations
   D. An attempt to substantially reduce the debt over the short run would decrease the money supply

      (1) All of these
      (2) A, B and D only
      (3) A and C only
      (4) B and D only
      (5) C and D only

4. A federal government can "demonetize the national debt" by

      (1) selling new bonds to banks to raise capital to pay off its existing debt
      (2) creating demand deposits to finance its debt
      (3) rescheduling the repayment of its debt to a time later than originally planned
      (4) reducing its debt with current revenues

ANALYSIS OF SAMPLE OBJECTIVE QUESTIONS

1. Choice (2) is the correct answer. Statements A, B, and C are all correct. According to a regressive rate structure, the tax rate decreases as the size of the tax base <u>increases</u>, so statement D is false.

2. The correct answer is choice (1). Choices (2), (3), and (4) are all incorrect. Under a deficit budget, the government spends more than it receives in taxes. Therefore, if the economy is at less than full employment, government spending will increase effective demand. (If the economy is at full employment, inflation will occur.) A surplus budget will decrease the level of economic activity (2) and serve as a fiscal drag on the economy (4). A balanced budget will have a neutral effect on the economy (3).

3. The correct answer is choice (4). Statements B and D are correct. Statement A is false because the taxation and repayment of the national debt causes only a redistribution of income, or cash assets. There is no reduction in the total income or assets of the nation. Statement C is wrong. In terms of the total economy, it is impossible to pass the real cost of the national debt on to future generations; the burden of the national debt for individuals and firms can be passed on.

4. Choice (4) is the correct answer. Choices (1), (2), and (3) are
    actions the government could take to monetize the debt; therefore,
    these three choices are all incorrect.

REVIEW QUESTIONS

1. The burden of many taxes tend to be shifted forward to the ultimate
    purchaser. Occasionally the effect is shifted backward. Give an
    example of each situation.

2. "A nation should postpone payment on the national debt, since the debt
    becomes less burdensome as the years go on." In what ways is this a
    good suggestion? A poor suggestion?

3. The U.S. Congress imposed a 4.25 percent ceiling on the interest rate
    that the Treasury can pay on long-term government securities. How
    does this Congressional action affect the efforts of the Treasury
    Department to refund the national debt?

18

International Trade and the Balance of Payments

OBJECTIVES

In this chapter, you will study free trade and the barriers nations erect against free trade. You will become acquainted with national and international organizations that assist trade. You will see how nations achieve a balance of payments in their current accounts. Upon completion of this chapter, you should be able to

- Identify the various barriers to free trade

- Summarize the arguments for and against free trade

- Explain the importance of the General Agreement on Tariffs and Trade

- Discuss the functions of the World Bank

- Indicate whether transactions are considered debits or credits on the international balance of accounts

- Describe the three types of exchange rates

- Explain the purpose of the International Monetary Fund

WORKING OUTLINE

I. INTERNATIONAL TRADE

1. Just as trade between various sections of a nation can improve

the welfare of all people involved, so too can trade between

nations benefit both _____.

2. The value of United States imports or exports is only about _____ percent of its large GNP, while Canadian exports in 1982 were _____ percent of its GNP.

3. Trade takes places as nations seek to improve _____ _____ and to take advantage of _____ _____.

4. Most of the international trade is carried on among developed nations since _____ _____.

Barriers to Free Trade

5. If economic arguments strongly favor free trade, why do most nations of the world invoke numerous restrictions in the area of international trade? _____ _____ _____.

The Tariff

6. A tariff is a duty or tax _____.

7. Define the following terms so as to differentiate between them:
   ● Specific tariff--_____
   ● Ad valorem tariff--_____

8. A tariff may be levied either for _____ or for _____.

9. For many years, the primary purpose of import duties was to

   _____

   _____ .

10. Later tariffs became a major tool used by countries to _____

    _____ .

11. To be effective, a tariff must serve one or the other of the
    aforementioned purposes, since they are to a large extent incom-
    patible. Explain. _____

    _____

    _____

12. Although there may be a(n) _____ which will
    serve both purposes, it cannot serve either purpose as well as a
    tariff designed with only one purpose in mind.

13. At present only a relatively small amount of income is derived
    from import duties, so it is difficult to support an argument
    that a tariff is essential to _____ .

14. The fundamental argument for free trade is that tariffs deny
    individuals and nations the _____
    and the _____ which result from
    the exercise of the laws of absolute and comparative advantage.

15. Tariffs disturb and restrict _____ ,
    eliminate _____ ,
    and prevent _____ .

16. Although the actual customs duty is levied on the _____,
ultimately all tariffs are paid by the _____.

17. Who are the main beneficiaries of a tariff? _____

_____

18. One of the oldest and most plausible of the arguments for tariffs
is _____.

- This argument was instrumental in promoting the shift in United
States and Canadian tariff policy from one of _____
to one of _____ in the early part of the
19th century.

19. Explain this argument. _____

_____

_____

_____

20. The true infant-industry protectionist maintains that the tariff
should be continued only until _____
_____. At that point, the
tariff should be removed and the domestic industry should be
forced to _____ or _____.

21. A similar argument is made for the _____ tariff
that is designed to equalize the _____ between
domestic and foreign producers.

337

22. Supposedly, this tariff removes any advantage to foreign producers arising from differences among countries in _____ _____, so that the cost (including _____) or price of both the foreign and domestic products would be equal.

  ● Consequently, this type of tariff would remove the fundamental benefit and reasons for _____.

23. It is often suggested that the use of tariffs creates or protects _____.

  ● If tariffs are imposed, _____ will be kept out of the domestic nation.

  ● Consumers will shift to the purchase of _____ _____, which will result in increased domestic _____ and _____.

24. This short-sighted argument takes into account only one side of international trade.

  ● Foreigners cannot continue to _____ unless they have that country's currency, and the primary way they obtain that currency is by _____.

  ● If tariffs are imposed and imports restricted, foreigners will have less of that country's _____ to buy _____.

  ● There will be a decrease in production and employment in _____.

25. A tariff brings about a transfer of income from _____

_____ to

_____ .

26. It is frequently argued that tariffs are necessary to _____

_____ United States and Canadian wage rates.

● Since many foreigners have lower wage rates than do United

   States and Canadian workers, it is contended that, if lower

   priced foreign goods are admitted into the nation, _____

   will force domestic producers to _____ , particularly

   _____ , in an effort to stay in business.

27. Why is this argument generally held to be untrue? _____

_____

_____

28. Even if the wage cost per unit were lower in some foreign in-

dustries, it would be a disservice to domestic consumers to

_____ the less _____ domestic producer

with a tariff.

29. One of the weakest arguments for tariffs is the proposal that it

keeps money _____ instead of _____ .

● Foreigners, however, use the dollars they receive from the sale

   of their imported goods to purchase _____

   _____ , so that the dollars

   return _____ .

● Most imports are _____, or _____, by

exports, so that very little money actually _____.

30. One of the strongest of the protectionist arguments for tariffs

is that tariffs will help _____.

● If tariffs are not established and maintained for industries

producing strategic defense materials, some of these industries

might have to _____.

● Then, if war breaks out, the domestic nation will be at a

distinct disadvantage in the production of military goods and

armaments if _____.

31. Some individuals argue that tariffs should be used to diversify

_____.

● What are the dangers to a country of specializing in the pro-

duction of one or a few commodities? _____

_____

_____

● Tariffs can be used to keep imports out of such a country and

to encourage _____.

● With a broader industrial structure, the economy will become

_____ and be _____

_____.

32. This last argument has some degree of validity, but it has

relatively little application to _____

which are known for their _____.

Quotas, Subsidies, and Exchange Controls

33. Nontariff barriers are used to grant _____ to _____

    _____. List three possible effects of non-

    tariff barriers.

    (1) _____

    (2) _____

    (3) _____

34. What is an <u>import quota</u>? _____

    _____

35. Identify and describe the two primary types of import quotas.

    (1) _____

    (2) _____

36. Quotas serve to protect the domestic producer and industry

    against _____.

37. Sometimes both a tariff and a quota are used, in which case the

    _____ that is imported is subject to

    _____.

38. What is a <u>tariff quota</u>? _____

    _____

    _____

39. The export subsidy is designed to encourage _____

or to prevent discrimination against exporters who may have to

_____

_____.

40. The flow of international trade can be affected greatly by the use of exchange controls.

● One such control is the rationing of _____

_____, which would limit the _____

_____.

41. More specific regulation of imports is possible through the use

of _____, which means that different

_____ are set for various commodities.

● In this manner the importation of some commodities can be encouraged while _____.

North American Trade Assistance

42. In the past decades, the United States and Canada have tried to

promote freer trade by _____

and by _____

_____.

43. In 1934, the United States federal government established the

_____, with a primary purpose of

financing _____ from the United States.

● Under certain conditions, the bank guarantees domestic

exporters that _____

_____.

342

- Sometimes the bank _____

  to buy United States goods.

- The bank mainly finances _____

  between the United States and other nations that cannot be

  _____

  _____.

44. In 1970, Canada established the _____

    to assist in the promotion of international trade.

    - The corporation provides a wide range of _____,

      _____, and _____ services to Canadian

      exporters and foreign buyers.

    - It reports to the Parliament through the _____

      _____.

General Agreement on Tariffs and Trade

45. The General Agreement on Tariffs and Trade (GATT) was drawn up at

    _____ in _____ by Allied nations who had met for

    the purpose of _____.

46. List four provisions of GATT.

    (1) _____

    (2) _____

    (3) _____

    (4) _____

47. Although more than 80 nations have adopted GATT, it is an in-
    formal agreement, so a nation cannot be compelled to _____

    _____.

Multilateral Trade Negotiations and the Tokyo Round, 1978

48. In the 1950s and 1960s, there was much progress toward the
    development of _____.

49. The promotion of international trade on a multilateral basis--
    that is, _____--was in-
    strumental in overall economic growth and the improvement in the
    standard of living in the world's three major industrial sectors,
    which are

    (1) _____ (3) _____

    (2) _____

50. Identify four factors which led to the 1970s slowdown in the
    movement toward free trade:

    (1) _____

    (2) _____

    (3) _____

    (4) _____

51. List three actions against free trade taken by the United States,
    Canada, and other nations.

    (1) _____

    (2) _____

    (3) _____

52. The Multilateral Trade Negotiations in 1978 were held as a result

of _____.

   ● The Tokyo Round of these negotiations led to the following four
     agreements:

     (1) _____

     (2) _____

     (3) _____

     (4) _____

   ● The negotiators also agreed on measures to improve the GATT

     framework for dealing with _____, _____

     _____, _____, and

     _____.

Aid Through International Organizations

53. The World Bank, formally known as the _____

   _____, is in-

   tended to _____

   _____.

54. What is a nation's subscription to the World Bank? _____

   _____

   _____

55. The World Bank can _____ and use the proceeds for

   _____, and it can _____.

345

56. The overall purpose of the bank is to develop _____

    _____

    _____ .

57. The objectives of the World Bank are predicated on the assumption

    that _____

    _____ .

58. What is the general objective of the International Finance

    Corporation (IFC)? _____

    _____

    _____

59. List the three proposals of the IFC for accomplishing this
    objective:

    (1) _____

    _____

    (2) _____

    _____

    (3) _____

60. The International Development Administration (IDA) was estab-

    lished to enable _____

    _____ .

    ● Development credits and loans are intended to impose _____

       _____ on the balance of payments of borrowing countries

       than do conventional loans.

II. THE BALANCE OF INTERNATIONAL PAYMENTS

1. International trade is encouraged by the disparities among the

   _____, _____, _____, and

   _____ in different countries.

2. Trade among various nations is promoted by businesses seeking to

   expand trade beyond _____

   and by a general lack of _____.

3. Therefore, payment must be made for _____

   _____ and nations must deal with the

   _____.

III. BALANCE OF TRADE

1. Some nations tend to export more than they import from other

   specific nations, and vice versa. In many cases of _____

   _____, however, a surplus against one nation may be

   offset by a deficit against another nation.

2. Define the following terms:

   ● Favorable balance of trade--_____

     _____

   ● Unfavorable balance of trade--_____

     _____

3. Explain why the term "favorable balance" is a misnomer.

   _____

   _____

4. What is the correlation between the economic development of a nation and the status of the balance of trade?

_____

_____

_____

Debits and Credits

5. International trade items are recorded as debits or credits on

   the _____.

6. A debit entry is made for transactions that give rise to

   _____ from any domestic

   _____, _____, or the _____.

7. The largest debit category arises from the _____

   of goods and services. In addition to commodities, this debit

   includes charges for _____, _____, _____,

   _____, and the like.

8. Another important debit category is capital outflow. Cite three examples of capital outflow.

   (1) _____

   (2) _____

   (3) _____

9. Debit entries are also made for unilateral transfers abroad,

   which arise as a result of _____, _____

   _____, _____, and similar one-way

   transactions.

● Large expenditures for _____ by the

government are included in this debit category.

10. What type of gold movement is considered a debit transaction in

the balance of payments? _____

_____

11. Credit transactions are the opposite of debit transactions and

give rise to _____ against _____, _____,

_____, and _____ of foreign nations.

12. List five examples of major credit items in the United States and
Canadian balance of payments.

(1) _____

(2) _____

(3) _____

(4) _____

(5) _____

13. Total debits must always equal credits. What three actions may
occur to make them balance?

(1) _____

(2) _____

(3) _____

IV. BALANCE OF PAYMENTS

1. The balance of payments designates whether a nation is going

to have either an inflow or outflow of _____

or the purchase or sale of _____.

2. Although the _____ is the largest category of international transactions, it is by no means the only segment that must be considered in determining whether or not a particular nation will have a positive or deficit balance of payments.

3. The dollar claims of the rest of the world against a particular nation result from that nation's importation of foreign goods and from the _____ among nations.

4. Prior to August 1971, how did the United States settle a deficit balance of payments? _____

_____

5. Currently, the United States settles deficits and surpluses through changes and adjustments in domestic and foreign assets, both government and private. Describe three such changes and adjustments that are sometimes made.

(1) _____

(2) _____

(3) _____

_____

6. Since a negative balance on current accounts is usually settled or eliminated by _____

_____ and occasionally by _____,

some international trade analysts object to the term _____

_____.

7. It should be remembered that a surplus or deficit is not nearly

   so important as is the _____.

V. FOREIGN EXCHANGE RATES

1. International sales are similar to domestic sales expect that

   _____

   _____

   _____. Consequently, a conversion

   must be made from _____ to _____

   to complete the transaction.

2. Banks dealing in foreign exchange maintain deposits in foreign
   banks to facilitate the conversion of currency.

   ● The domestic bank accepts domestic currency and gives a bank
     draft for foreign currency.

   ● The foreign bank then honors that draft and reduces the

     _____ of the domestic bank.

3. Many foreign trade transactions can be paid by _____

   without necessarily involving a large _____.

4. Currency exchange rates play an important role in international

   economics because a particular exchange rate may _____

   _____

5. A change in the exchange rate may actually reverse _____

   _____.

6. The three types of exchange rates are:

(1) _____ (3) _____

(2) _____

Flexible Exchange Rates

7. When exchange rates are determined by the free forces of supply

and demand, they will fluctuate with changes in _____

_____ and the consequent changes in

_____

_____.

8. The term that is commonly used to refer to an exchange rate that

is not fixed is _____.

* * * * * *

Statements 9 through 14 below pertain to the international trade
between two countries, Epsilon and Upsilon, that have a flexible
exchange rate and a certain balance of payments.

9. Assume that, for some reason, there is a sharp increase in demand
for Epsilon dollars in the country of Upsilon.

10. If the Epsilon dollar becomes scarce relative to Upsilon dollars

in the Upsilon foreign exchange markets, the price of the Epsilon

dollar in Upsilon may _____.

11. In light of the relationship between the two currencies, citizens
of Upsilon now find it less attractive to purchase goods and
services from Epsilon.

12. Consumers in Epsilon now find it advantageous to purchase Upsilon goods and services rather than goods and services produced domestically in Epsilon.

13. What happens to the demand for Upsilon dollars in Epsilon foreign exchange markets? _____

14. What happens to the price of Upsilon dollars relative to the price of Epsilon dollars? _____

_____

* * * * * *

15. Flexible exchange rates serve as a means of correcting _____

_____.

Fixed Exchange Rates

16. Under the gold standard, which was a common method for establishing fixed exchange rates in the earlier part of this century, nations defined _____ in terms of gold and permitted the _____ of gold, as well as the freedom to import and export, as a means of

_____.

17. Under the gold standard, exchange rates between two currencies were based on the value, in gold, of each currency.

18. The gold points were the fixed exchange rate plus and minus the cost of _____.

19. If the exchange rate rose above or fell below the gold points, merchants would find it less costly to ship gold in payment for goods than to purchase an exchange draft.

20. The flow of gold from one nation to another would set in motion

    forces that would alter the exchange rate and reverse the

    _____.

21. List two reasons why this method is no longer used as a means of fixing exchange rates.

    (1) _____

    (2) _____

Controlled or Managed Exchange Rates

22. With the abandonment of the gold standard in the 1930s, many

    nations either _____ or

    _____ immediately.

23. What does a nation hope to avoid by controlling the exchange

    rate? _____

    _____

24. Exchange control usually involves a government agreement to main-

    tain a particular exchange rate between _____

    and _____.

25. To maintain that rate of exchange, a government must be prepared

    to _____ as the market

    price deviates up and down.

26. A nation with a managed currency usually establishes an "exchange

stabilization fund" composed of _____,

_____, and _____ used for

buying and selling foreign exchange.

27. Exchange controls may be _____ in nature insofar as

one nation may determine the rate at which it desires to

stabilize the exchange rate between itself and other nations.

● If such a rate works to the detriment of other nations,

exchange-rate competition or retaliation may ensue and give

rise to _____.

● What safeguard has been established to avert this possibility?

_____

_____

_____

28. Exchange rates may be managed to an even greater degree by any

nation through _____

_____.

This, in turn, limits the total demand for _____

and influences the _____.

VI. INTERNATIONAL MONETARY FUND

1. In 1944, the International Monetary Fund (IMF) was established in

an attempt to stabilize _____ and to provide

_____

_____.

Establishing Exchange Rates

2. Each member of the IMF established a par value for its currency
    in terms of _____ or _____.

3. The IMF established international exchange rates and members were
    charged with an obligation to maintain their _____
    _____ within _____.

Assistance to Members

4. Each member nation was assigned _____
    _____ which it had to contribute to the IMF.

    ● List three factors on which the quota was primarily based:

     (1) _____ (3) _____

     (2) _____

    ● At least 25 percent of the subscription had to be paid in

     _____ (or _____

     _____) and the remainder in _____

     _____.

5. With the existence of the IMF, any particular nation that has a
    deficit balance of payments or a shortage of foreign exchange
    should not be required to _____, as
    was the case under the gold standard, or to _____
    _____, as experienced under the individually
    controlled exchange rate system, in an attempt to obtain relief.

6. The mechanism of the IMF was originally designed to prevent

   _____ that could come about under a system of

   freely fluctuating exchange rates.

7. How can a member nation that has a shortage of a particular type

   of foreign exchange obtain temporary relief? _____

   _____

8. One of the main functions of the IMF is the administration of

   Special Drawing Rights (SDRs). What are SDRs? _____

   _____

   _____

9. How would a country with a balance-of-payments deficit use SDRs

   to settle its account? _____

   _____

   _____

10. Nations with balance-of-payments surpluses may _____

    _____ much as they

    would accumulate gold reserves.

11. Nations that continuously experience _____

    _____ or _____ and

    whose difficulty cannot be corrected by _____

    _____ may have to seek other remedies.

12. Any member nation may change its exchange rate by 10 percent

merely by _____; any further devaluation

must have _____.

Experience of the IMF

13. The IMF has met with only modest success in its 40 years of

operations.

14. Since its primary function is to offer _____

_____

rather than to offer _____

_____, it will necessarily

function better in a more stable international situation than in

one replete with serious monetary crises.

TERMINOLOGY AND CONCEPTS INTRODUCED

tariff--_____

_____

specific tariff--_____

_____

ad valorem tariff--_____

_____

nontariff barriers--_____

_____

import quota--_____

_____

global quota--_____

_____

allocated quota--_____

_____

tariff quota--_____

_____

export subsidy--_____

_____

exchange controls--_____

_____

favorable balance of trade--_____

_____

unfavorable balance of trade--_____

_____

deficit balance of payments--_____

_____

floating rate--_____

_____

gold points--_____

_____

Special Drawing Rights (SDRs)--_____

_____

SAMPLE OBJECTIVE QUESTIONS

1. There are several types of taxes levied on foreign imports. One such
    tax is set at a given percentage of the value of each unit imported.
    This type of tax is called

        (1) a tariff quota
        (2) a specific tariff
        (3) an ad valorem tariff
        (4) an allocated tariff

2. Among the arguments often given in support of a policy of free trade, and against a system of protective tariffs, are that tariffs

   A. Protect only new or infant industries
   B. Prevent the optimum use of scarce factors of production
   C. Deny individuals and nations the gains that can be enjoyed from the exercise of the laws of absolute and comparative advantage
   D. Tend to benefit mainly the relatively inefficient producers

      (1) All of these
      (2) A, B and C only
      (3) A, C and D only
      (4) B, C and D only
      (5) B and D only

3. The Canadian organization which provides a wide range of guarantee, loan, and insurance services to Canadian exporters and foreign buyers is the

      (1) Export Development Corporation
      (2) Federal Business Development Bank
      (3) Bank for Reconstruction and Development
      (4) Economic Council of Canada

4. The following types of economic transactions usually are classified as debits in a country's international balance of accounts:

   A. Expenditures by the country's government for foreign aid
   B. The purchase of foreign securities
   C. A direct investment abroad by the country's government
   D. The exportation of gold from within the country

      (1) All of these
      (2) A, B and C only
      (3) A and B only
      (4) A and D only
      (5) C and D only

5. For any nation using a flexible or floating rate of currency exchange in conducting international trade, the actual rate of exchange at a given time is determined by the

      (1) difference between the number of gold points set for the currency of the nation and the number of gold points set for the currency of the trading partner
      (2) amount of gold or silver that the nation holds, compared to the amount a trading partner holds
      (3) forces of supply and demand as reflected by fluctuations in the nation's exports and imports
      (4) amount of the nation's Special Drawing Rights in connection with the nation's account with the International Monetary Fund

ANALYSIS OF SAMPLE OBJECTIVE QUESTIONS

1. Choice (3) is the correct answer. A tariff quota (1) is a trade barrier that allows a certain amount of a commodity to come in at one tariff rate, but charges a higher tariff rate for any additional units of the commodity. A specific tariff (2) is a set amount of tax levied on each unit imported. A quota is described as an <u>allocated</u> quota (4) if it assigns different import limits to different importers.

2. The correct answer is choice (4). Statements B, C, and D are all true. Statement A is false because tariffs can protect all domestic industries, not only infant industries.

3. The correct answer is choice (1). The Federal Business Development Bank (2) assists the development of new or existing business enterprises in Canada. The <u>International</u> Bank for Reconstruction and Development (3) is another name for the World Bank. The Economic Council of Canada (4) is an advisory body that assists in the formulation of Canadian macroeconomic policies.

4. Choice (2) is the correct answer; statements A, B, and C are true. Statement D is false because an inflow of gold from abroad is a debit transaction; gold exports is an example of a credit transaction.

5. Choice (3) is the correct answer. When a nation has a flexible exchange rate, the determination of the exchange rate has nothing to do with gold and silver stores (2), or gold points (1), or Special Drawing Rights (4).

REVIEW QUESTIONS

1. Use an example to illustrate the process whereby the government pays an export subsidy.

2. Explain fully the objections of some international trade analysts to the use of the term <u>deficit balance of payments</u>. Explain also the justification for this term given by those who use it.

3. Describe in detail the process whereby payment is made for the purchase of foreign goods and services.

4. When two nations are under the gold standard, the flow of gold from one nation to the other sets in motion forces that cause changes in the exchange rate and reverse the outflow of gold. Describe this process.

5. How does a government maintain a controlled exchange rate?

6. How have the events of the past 40 years prevented the IMF from achieving anything more than modest success?